STIRLING MOSS
MY RACING LIFE

MY RACING LIFE

Sir Stirling Moss
with Simon Taylor

[signature]

This book is one of 150
limited editions signed
at the launch at the
Royal Automobile Club,
Pall Mall, 30th April 2015

[signature]

Published in May 2015

ISBN 978-1-910505-06-9

Published by Evro Publishing
Westrow House, Holwell, Sherborne, Dorset DT9 5LF

Printed and bound in China by 1010 Printing International Ltd

Every effort has been made to trace and acknowledge holders of copyright in photographs and to obtain their permission for the use of photographs. The publisher apologises for any errors or omissions in the credits given throughout this book and would be grateful to be notified of any corrections that should be incorporated in future reprints or editions.

Designed by Richard Parsons
Photo research by Mark Hughes
With thanks to Mandy Shepherd

www.evropublishing.com

Publisher's acknowledgements
Evro Publishing would like to thank the following suppliers of photographs: LAT (Kathy Ager, Steve Carpenter, Kevin Wood and Tim Wright), Getty Images, Klemantaski Collection (Peter Sachs), Guy Griffiths Collection (Michael Hammond), Ferret Fotographics (Ted Walker), Pete Lyons (for the work of Ozzie Lyons), Daimler Archive (for Mercedes-Benz photos), BRDC Archive (Steph Sykes-Dugmore), Sutton Images (Keith Sutton and Annie Lydon), TopFoto (Flora Smith), Rex Features (Stephen Atkinson), National Motor Museum (Jon Day), The Revs Institute for Automotive Research, Terry Marshall, Geoff Cowen, Paul Skilleter and Maurice Rowe.

Jacket photographs
Front: British Grand Prix, Aintree, 1955 (Rex Features)
Back, clockwise from top left: Kieft, Brands Hatch, 1952 (LAT); Jaguar D-type, Tourist Trophy, Dundrod, 1954 (Ferret Fotographics); Vanwall, Pescara Grand Prix, 1957 (LAT); Lotus 18, Monaco Grand Prix, 1961 (LAT)

STIRLING MOSS
MY RACING LIFE

STIRLING MOSS WITH SIMON TAYLOR

FOREWORD
LEWIS HAMILTON

CONTENTS

FOREWORD
LEWIS HAMILTON

I am delighted to have this opportunity to pay tribute to Sir Stirling Moss by writing a foreword to his new book.

Ever since I became fascinated by motor sport as a young boy I knew, as everybody else did, the name of Stirling Moss. He is considered by many to be the greatest British racing driver of all time. Of course I was never able to see him race during his professional career, but that didn't stop him from being one of the motivations that drove me on to reach the top of the motor racing tree for my country.

Stirling had one of his finest Formula 1 seasons driving for Mercedes-Benz. I have now won my second World Championship for Mercedes-Benz. It was great to be able to line our cars up side by side and compare them, the W196 and the W05 Hybrid, designed 60 years apart and technically more different than you could imagine. I told Stirling I couldn't dream of racing his car. He said he couldn't dream of racing mine. But they were both made to chase precisely the same goal: to beat the rest of the world. And that's what they both did.

As this book shows, motor racing was very different in the 1950s. Stirling raced all sorts of different types of car, often on the same day. The total team behind his racing efforts was sometimes three or four people. Today a Formula 1 driver concentrates on Formula 1, with a team of more than 1000 people working together, inventing, developing and putting to competitive use some of the most ground-breaking technology the world has ever seen – but still, once again, with that identical goal: to win.

Winning one's home Grand Prix is always the most special of all race victories. Stirling, the first Briton to do it, won it twice. I have now won it twice, and I hope I'll do it again. That's one of the things that allows Stirling and me to compare notes and swap stories.

I would like to say that Sir Stirling is an amazing man with huge character and charisma. Still today, at 85 years of age, he is sharper than most and carries his wit in style. I am honoured to be able to say he is my friend.

This book demonstrates the full variety of how much Stirling Moss achieved, in just 14 seasons. I hope you enjoy it.

PREFACE
SIMON TAYLOR

The name Stirling Moss has been part of the country's consciousness for more than half a century. When you carve up somebody in traffic, the angry voice that shouts after you doesn't say, 'Who do you think you are? James Hunt?' Or '…Jackie Stewart?' It still says, 'Who do you think you are? Stirling Moss?' It's as though he has become public property, a national treasure.

Except that, unlike many other heroes, a famous footballer, say, or a rock star, he feels he has a duty to be friendly. In the days when we had phone directories, he was never ex-directory. If he is recognised in the street and asked for an autograph or – increasingly nowadays – a selfie, he is patient and courteous. At events like the Goodwood Revival or the Monaco Historics, when he is surrounded by more knowledgeable fans, he will answer their questions in an interested, involved way, not dismissively, even though he may have answered the same question countless times. And the fan will go away cherishing the fact that he or she has had a conversation with Stirling Moss.

When I was a motor-racing-mad schoolboy, 60 years or more ago, of course he was my hero. Almost as soon as I could read, I devoured tales of his exploits in my father's car magazines every week. I wrote him a letter, asking for his autograph. Six days later I got a friendly reply on Stirling Moss headed paper, enclosing an original photograph of him drifting an Aston Martin DB3S through Madgwick, signed in ink.

I still have my history exercise book from my boarding school. In the front are notes about the Civil War, Oliver Cromwell and the Restoration. In the back, the record I kept of my hero's season: 1958 – 38 races, retired 14, finished 24, won 18. My calculations in the margin show that was a success rate, when the car got him to the end of the race, of 75 per cent.

In 1956, aged 11, I persuaded my father to take me to the Easter Monday Goodwood (see page 152). Enthralled, I watched Stirling's 250F Maserati battle with Mike Hawthorn's BRM and Archie Scott Brown's Connaught, and win. By the 1962 Easter Monday meeting I was 17, and old enough to drive myself in my newly acquired £80 Austin van to Goodwood. I decided to watch from the St Mary's grandstand. On lap 35 of the Glover Trophy, the entire stand gave a sort of universal gasp and jumped to its feet. This blocked my view, but it was clear Stirling had crashed, Stirling was badly hurt. As my old van struggled home to Somerset I was distraught. In the days that followed, like most of the country, I listened to the hourly radio bulletins about his condition. The BBC gave it the same priority as the approaching death of an elder statesman, or a serious illness in the royal family.

A few years later, now working as a junior motor racing journalist, I often saw Stirling because he was very much part of the establishment, and came to most of the big meetings. But I was too much in awe of him to introduce myself. Then one day he sent me a polite letter commenting on something I had written, whether in criticism or praise I do not remember. Gradually we got to know each other.

At once I discovered two things about him. First, his unbelievable energy drove him as fast as ever, and it was very difficult to keep up with him. Second, I learned that Stirling is a modest man. It is not a false modesty – he does realise that he was the best racing driver of his era – but there is not a trace of arrogance or self-importance. When he was knighted in 2000 he was surprised but, as a staunch patriot, he was deeply gratified. His courtesy belongs to a former era. He automatically displays, alike to people he knows and to people he has never met, that old-fashioned trait which used to be called Good Manners.

In 1995 I suggested that he celebrate the 40th anniversary

of his Mille Miglia win by asking Mercedes to lend him the 722 300SLR for the three-day Retrospective, and get Denis Jenkinson to go with him. Next day he was on the phone. 'Jenks doesn't want to come. He says he did the real thing, and why should he ponce around with rich old men in their shiny Ferraris. You'd better come instead, boy.'

My time with Stirling in Italy was unforgettable. Over the mountain passes and across the plains, whenever the cheering crowds stood back enough to allow it, he drove the SLR not *quite* as fast as it would go, but almost. My days as a star-struck schoolboy were gone. Now Stirling was a friend, and over dinner, or waiting in line to drive into a control because we'd arrived too early, he told me countless stories of his racing life. Not as I'd read them in the magazines, but as they had really happened, from his own point of view.

I've been able to count him as a friend ever since. His wonderful wife Susie has become a good friend too, and my wife Pearl and I have spent a lot of time with them, travelling to

↑ In the 1995 Mille Miglia I spent three unforgettable days alongside Stirling in the 300SLR. His smooth, fluid, apparently effortless driving style was a revelation to me, and evidently unchanged since he averaged almost 100mph for 1000 miles in this very car in the real race in 1955.
📷 *LAT*

events abroad, laughing a lot, and hearing yet more of Stirling's stories. This book has grown out of that. Stirling decided to get out his diaries and his scrapbooks, look again at the photographs, and show me what was happening in each one. He wanted to tell the tales again, and he wanted me to write them down. For me it has been a very great privilege.

During his career the media called him Mr Motor Racing. It's more than 50 years since his professional racing career ended against that earth bank at St Mary's, but for me he will always remain exactly that. I hope this book will show you why.

CHAPTER 1
CHILDHOOD

I was born barely three months before the end of the 1920s, on 17 September 1929. In those days motor racing was mainly the preserve of the well-to-do amateur, and as I went through my childhood I don't think it occurred to me that I would ever be able to earn my living at it. However, cars certainly played their part in my family. As soon as World War I was over my father Alfred, who was a dentist, did hillclimbs in an AV Bicar and raced a Crouch at Brooklands. Then in his late 20s he travelled to America and shrewdly enrolled in the dentistry school at the University of Indiana, because it was on the doorstep of the famous Indianapolis Speedway.

Having somehow persuaded the US racing establishment that he was a top driver from Europe, he wangled a drive in the 1924 Indianapolis 500 in one of Louis Chevrolet's Fronty-Fords. Chevrolet was no longer part of the famous car manufacturer he'd founded, and his Frontenac Motor Corporation was making overhead-cam conversions for the good old sidevalve Ford four-cylinder. It wasn't exactly the latest or most competitive car, but Dad finished 16th and won himself $900, quite a sum then. As a result of that he was offered more drives by Chevrolet, travelling around the country to race on dirt tracks for the rest of the season.

My grandfather wasn't too happy at the prospect of Dad becoming an American fairground racer, so he persuaded him to come back to England, and set him up in a garage business in Thornton Heath with his brother-in-law. But after a couple of years with that he went back to dentistry full-time. However, he did build a Fronty-Ford of his own, using a highly modified Model T chassis and Chevrolet-headed engine. It scored a win at the 1925 Brooklands August meeting, lapping at 85mph and causing a bit of excitement when the exhaust caught fire as he crossed the finish line.

It was at Brooklands that he first met my mother, a Scottish lady named Aileen Craufurd. She competed successfully in rallies and trials, and driving an overhead-cam Singer Sports she won the Ladies' Trials Championship. She moved on to a supercharged Marendaz, which was very dashing but not very reliable. She wanted me to be called Hamish, but my father thought perhaps that was too Scottish, so I was called Stirling after the town of her birth: Stirling Craufurd Moss.

When I was about five Dad drove me round Brooklands, and I remember getting burned bending over a hot exhaust pipe. Perhaps the scars on my tummy represented a sort of baptism. He was very keen on physical fitness, and from when I was very young he had me rope-climbing, boxing, swimming, rowing and the rest of it. And riding: my mother was also an accomplished horsewoman, and when I was only six she taught me to ride.

Over the next few years I won plenty of rosettes and trophies in gymkhanas and show-jumping, which sometimes carried useful prize money too. That went towards my savings for my first car, because I was already planning for that. I was always very competitive in everything I did: I liked to win, I didn't like to lose. Riding also gave me an understanding of balance and control from an early age, and no doubt that helped me subconsciously when I started to try to drive cars as fast as they would go.

My sister Pat, who was five years younger than me, went on to be a very successful horsewoman and a member of the British Show-jumping Team. In the 1950s and '60s she became a brilliant rally driver too, joining the works teams of successively BMC, Ford, Lancia and Renault. In those days it wasn't really done for a mere girl to beat all the top men, but beat them she did, winning some major international events outright.

From an early age I was always very competitive in everything I did: I liked to win, I didn't like to lose.

My father did well as a dentist, building up a large chain of practices. We moved to a house at Bray, near the River Thames, called Long White Cloud, which had some land with it where Dad did a bit of farming. For £15 he bought an old Austin 7 that was meant to help with chores around the farm, but soon the bodywork was stripped off, and by the time I was about 10 I was driving it as fast as it would go around the fields and up and down a steep dip behind the house. On grass that old thing taught me my first lessons in understeer and oversteer, and it was the first motor vehicle I ever drove – apart from sitting on Mum's lap when I was even younger, steering her Lancia Aprilia up and down the drive.

So I had a pretty happy childhood. I went to prep school in Berkshire, which I enjoyed, and to public school at Haileybury, which I didn't much. Academic work bored me, although I loved sports. World War II broke out when I was 10, and lasted until I was almost 16. I remember the air-raid sirens, and the German bombers coming over. Dad designed and patented the Morrison Shelter, which was a metal frame that went over your bed, to protect you in case your house was bombed and collapsed over you. I think about half a million were made and distributed, although he never made a penny out of the idea.

Having finished with school I was expected to pursue a career, and without quite knowing why I became a trainee hotel manager. I had to learn how to be everything from a night porter to a waiter to a washer-upper, and I don't think I was very good at any of it. Then I did a spell as a labourer on my father's farm – which meant getting up very early every morning.

My first car, when I was 16, was a Morgan three-wheeler, and then came an MG Midget. In 1947 my father bought a BMW 328, and let me borrow it for a few trials and rallies. On 2 March 1947 I won my very first pot on four wheels as opposed to four legs,

the Cullen Trophy in a Harrow Car Club trial. Then I won a 1st Class Award in the Junior Car Club's Eastbourne Rally. The first speed event I did was in September at the traditional Brighton Speed Trials, where two cars drive in a straight line from a standing start along the seafront down Madeira Drive. I only managed seventh in class there, but of course there were no corners to go round. The following weekend at Lytchett Manor, on a more interesting course, I was fourth in class.

Wandering around the paddock at Lytchett I could look at lots of exciting machinery, including ERA, Alta, pre-war Grand Prix Alfa Romeo and Bugatti Type 59. But what really caught my attention were the cars built to the new 500cc single-seater formula. Some were home-built 'specials', but the most professional-looking were the little Coopers driven by John Cooper and Eric Brandon, with rear-mounted JAP engines. The two Coopers ran in four classes going up to three times their engine size, and they won all four. That gave me something to think about on the way home to Long White Cloud.

Dad had always been adamant that no son of his was going to be a racing driver, but soon after the Lytchett Manor outing I persuaded him to accompany me in the BMW down to Surbiton 'just to have a look' at the Cooper garage, where the latest model, the Cooper Mk II, was sitting gleaming in the front window.

It turned out that Dad and Charles Cooper, John's father, had known each other before the war. Charles had been mechanic to top Brooklands driver Kaye Don, so they got on well. After a lot of talk, and plenty of propaganda from me, we left Surbiton with Dad having been persuaded that we should order a new Cooper Mk II, which would be built up for us over the winter. I could scarcely contain myself with the knowledge that in 1948 I was going to become a real racing driver.

⬆ As well as being a talented horsewoman, Mum was an accomplished rally driver. In this Singer Sports she won a lot of awards, and the Ladies' Trials Championship.
📷 *Stirling Moss collection*

⬅ Dad raced this Anzani-engined Crouch at the Easter Brooklands in 1923, and won the Private Competitors' Handicap. He was 26 years old then. His exploits in the Indianapolis 500 came the following year.
📷 *LAT*

← With Judy, my little chestnut pony, being presented with an early gymkhana trophy. On horseback I began to learn that coming first felt good, although I soon hankered after competing on four wheels rather than four legs.

📷 *Stirling Moss collection*

→ It was the fashion then to be photographed surrounded by one's winnings. Pat soon began to collect a lot as well, so we put all our horse trophies and some of my early motor racing cups together for this snap.

📷 *Stirling Moss collection*

← My first proper car was this Morgan three-wheeler, with Matchless V-twin engine hung on the front. It cost me £50. A three-wheeler without reverse gear counted as a motorcycle combination, which meant I could drive it legally at 16. I drove it flat-out everywhere, and once, when the single rear tyre burst, I turned it over.

📷 *Stirling Moss collection*

← My first four-wheeler was a TB-series MG Midget with a rather smart drophead body by Tickford, wind-up windows and all. It was more weatherproof than the Morgan, and therefore a better proposition for taking girls out. My life-long interest in crumpet had already begun.

📷 *Stirling Moss collection*

➔ I will always remember Sylvia with great fondness, because she first taught me what life was really about. However, I also remember a difficult moment when Mum came home unexpectedly while I was in the middle of one of her lessons.

📷 *Stirling Moss collection*

➔ This girl, according to my scrapbook of the time, was called Marlene, but she can't have been as good a teacher as Sylvia, because I don't remember very much about her.

📷 *Stirling Moss collection*

⬆ I was always very keen on all sports, except for cricket, which I regarded as a slow-moving bore. At school I boxed, rowed and did athletics, especially sprinting – which stood me in good stead later for Le Mans starts. And I always liked rugby, playing wing three-quarter. This is the team photograph for the Thames Valley Rugby Club for the 1949–50 season. I was already racing in Formula 3 by then, but I liked to keep active during the winter too. I am in the top row on the left, next to the team secretary.

📷 *Courtesy of Maidenhead (Thames Valley) Rugby Club*

⬆ In 1947, when I was 17, Dad bought a secondhand BMW 328 two-seater in green, a really first-rate sports car with the high-camshaft straight six that went on to become the post-war Bristol engine. Dad allowed me to use it for my first speed events, like the Brighton Speed Trials. This straight-line event relied on horsepower only, so the best I could do was seventh in class.
📷 *Guy Griffiths Collection*

⬅ More challenging was this sprint at Lytchett Manor, near Poole, a half-mile course that included a fast left-hander and a tight S-bend. I finished fourth in my class behind an HRG and two more BMW 328s driven by well-known racers Anthony Crook (who I raced against some years later) and Betty Haig.
📷 *Guy Griffiths Collection*

CHAPTER 2
COOPERS AND KIEFTS

In recent years cheap single-seater classes for young hopefuls starting out in motor racing, Formula Ford and the like, have become two a penny. So it's hard to imagine the huge impact the new Formula 3 had on motor racing just after the war. The rules were pretty simple: a 500cc engine – almost everyone used single-cylinder air-cooled motorcycle units – in a small, light chassis. To start with there were lots of different manufacturers trying to make their mark, but before long Cooper almost had a monopoly.

Our BMW was sold, for £1000, and that provided the funds for my new Cooper, painted cream. It cost £575 without engine and some necessary spares, and we got its JAP engine from Stan Greening of J.A. Prestwich at a good deal, mainly because Dad did his teeth. The first meeting on my calendar was the Shelsley Walsh hillclimb on 2 May 1948, but when I sent in my entry they hadn't heard of me, and sent it back.

For the Prescott hillclimb the following weekend I got accepted, so I suppose that was the real start of my racing career. A few days before I'd driven the car for the first time, completely illegally, on the roads around a new housing estate being built near Slough – until an old lady on a bicycle wobbled across in front of me and I had to swerve onto the verge to avoid her. No damage, off to Prescott, and I posted fourth in class. I scored my first class win at Stanmer Park a week later.

My first actual race came at Brough in July, on a little track using part of a wartime airfield near Hull. In pouring rain I won my heat and the final, and also a handicap race after starting at the back. I was gratified to see coverage in the *Daily Mail*, under the headline *Brough Race Won by Back Marker*. Even more gratifying was my prize money of £13.

At Goodwood in September I won again, but at the first-ever Silverstone meeting I was leading when the engine sprocket came loose. Nevertheless, things had gone pretty well that first season: 15 outings, 11 wins. My father, having been so hard to persuade in the beginning, was now totally supportive and was on hand in his white overalls at every event, supported by our faithful German mechanic Donatus Müller. He was a prisoner of war who, when peace came, opted to stay in England. Before the war he had worked as a fitter for BMW.

I continued with these little rear-engined cars for seven seasons through to 1954. By then I was racing in Formula 1 in a Maserati 250F, and doing sports car and saloon racing in works Jaguars, plus rallies in works Sunbeams as well. But there was nothing to say you couldn't keep on in Formula 3 even if you were moving further up the ladder, and I always liked to do as much motor racing as I possibly could. Later on, in the bigger British meetings, I'd sometimes do five races in a day: Formula 1, big sports cars, small sports cars, touring cars, Formula 3.

Cooper updated and improved their cars each year, and for 1949 we had a longer-wheelbase Mk III, which would also take a JAP 1000cc twin to run in a different class. We got quite good at changing engines and sprockets, and in the same meeting we'd do a Formula 3 race with the 500cc single, then get down to a quick engine swap in the paddock and run in a Formula 2 or *formule libre* race later in the afternoon. We had the Mk III's aluminium bodywork anodised pale green, because we'd discovered that our methanol fuel stripped off the paint on the Mk II, and we had a horseshoe painted on the side for luck, with seven nail holes because that was my mother's lucky number – she was born on 7.7.1897. It became my lucky number too, and we always asked race organisers for number 7, or if we couldn't have that we'd go for 17, because I was born on 17 September.

In 1949 we ventured abroad for the first time, to Lake Garda in Italy where I used the 1000cc engine. I got £50 start money, and won £200 when my little Cooper won its class and finished third overall behind two Ferraris. Then Reims the next weekend, and on to Jersey for the Bouley Bay Hillclimb. Another week later, with the 500cc engine back in, we were off to Holland for Zandvoort, where I won again. Four events in four countries in 21 days, with start money and prize money, so racing was becoming pretty full-time for me now, and I was beginning to feel like a professional.

For 1950 we took our new Mk IV Cooper to Monaco, where I won the race supporting the Grand Prix. I was now racing a works HWM in Formula 2 around Europe, but that year I still managed to fit in 22 Formula 3 races.

The Norton twin overhead-cam engine, known in impolite circles as the 'double-knocker', was much more powerful than the JAP, but it was hard to get hold of. Nortons had developed it for their own motorcycle racing efforts and weren't bothered about seeing it on four wheels. It took us until August 1950 to get our double-knocker, and it was an immediate winner. On the Silverstone Grand Prix circuit I earned pole position by about three seconds; then the clutch packed up, and I got a push start after the rest of the grid had left. Even so I was in the lead by lap 2, and won easily.

That year I won my first BRDC Gold Star, and there were mutterings from some traditionalists because a lot of the points I'd scored had been in 500s. But it was a very competitive class, and because of their comparative lack of power the cars had to be carefully set-up and driven with great precision. Formula 3 certainly taught me a lot.

For 1951 Cyril Kieft wanted me to race one of his Kiefts but, even though I'd driven one the previous November to set some 350cc and 500cc speed records at Montlhéry, I didn't think they were up to much. So I suggested that Ray Martin, who'd done a great job of modifying my Mk IV Cooper to take the Norton engine, should build our ideal of a Formula 3 car and call it a Kieft. John *'Autocar'* Cooper – the journalist, not the race car builder – came up with a design that was far more sophisticated than any other Formula 3 car of the time, and the idea was that this would be a development car for the next production Kieft, with Cyril paying us a royalty on each one sold. It was a winner from the start, setting pole positions and smashing lap records with ease, although it did break a few times – including at the Nürburgring, where I was leading by 40 seconds when a steering arm snapped. Then in the 1952 Brussels GP there was a multiple pile-up, I turned over trying to avoid it, and others cannoned into my wreck. That wrote off the Kieft for good.

So it was back to Coopers, and in 1953 I had a lot of success in my new Mk VII. For 1954 I used a lightweight Cooper-based car built up by Francis Beart: it was the last season when I would be able to fit in Formula 3 races along with everything else, for in 1955 I would be a works Mercedes-Benz driver in Grands Prix and sports car races. But the 500cc Formula 3 had served me very well. Since my very first outing at Prescott six years before I'd done, according to my diaries, over 80 events in these little cars, and won more than 50 of them. Not a bad hit rate.

← My first ever event with the Cooper was at the Prescott Hillclimb in May 1948, when I got fourth in class. This shot at the Esses is on my return to Prescott two months later, when I won the class in 49.51s and was the only 500 driver to beat 50 seconds. It was particularly pleasing because three days before, at the Bouley Bay hillclimb in Jersey, the engine had blown up. Don Müller took the Cooper back to England on the ferry while Dad and I flew home and rushed around collecting the parts needed for the rebuild. Back then we used to tow the Cooper to events in a horse trailer behind Dad's old Rolls-Royce shooting brake, and that day Don and I travelled to Prescott in the bouncing, swaying trailer with the car, tearing the engine down and rebuilding it.

📷 *Ferret Fotographics*

⬇ My first class win came in my second event with the Cooper at the Stanmer Park hillclimb, near Brighton, after a great battle with Eric Brandon's works Cooper, which I finally beat by half a second. The track was very dusty, and this is me getting on the opposite lock to keep out of the straw bales. I was still wearing my basic black motorcycle helmet at this stage: helmets were not yet compulsory, but Dad forced me to wear one, which I thought was a bit sissy. I didn't wear gloves at first, either. This was the meeting when Bob Gerard, having set fastest time of day, couldn't stop his ERA after crossing the finish line and crashed into some parked cars and a tree. The meeting was abandoned after that, and I don't think the course was used again.

📷 *Stirling Moss collection*

↑ On 18 September 1948, the day after my 19th birthday, the first event was held at the new Goodwood track. It was my second proper circuit race meeting. I started mid-grid – positions were decided by ballot rather than practice times – but I soon got into the lead and won by 9.4 seconds from Eric Brandon.

📷 *LAT*

↗ By 1949 we were beginning to go to overseas races in France, Italy and Switzerland, where the organisers often paid start money to English visitors. In July we were among the sand dunes at the Dutch circuit of Zandvoort for a 10-lapper supporting the Dutch Grand Prix. I qualified on the front row, and when the flag fell the mechanic working on John Habin's car, next to me on the grid, was still on the track. As I started to move he stepped back into the path of my front wheel and cartwheeled over my car to land on the track behind me, whereupon he was run over by another car. I thought he must have been injured or even killed and came past the pits prepared to stop, but Dad frantically waved me on, so I decided he must be all right, caught up everybody else, got through the traffic and won the race.

📷 *Stirling Moss collection*

→ I had a busy 20th birthday at the 1949 Autumn Goodwood, entering the Mk III in 1000cc V-twin guise for three races. I won the first with no problem, setting fastest lap, but then in the second I suddenly couldn't select any gears. So John Cooper lent me his car for the third – but that failed after two laps. This paddock shot shows our little équipe: Dad, Mum and Don Müller.

📷 *Stirling Moss collection*

⬆ The first-ever round of the new Formula 1 World Championship was the British Grand Prix – also called the European Grand Prix – at Silverstone on 13 May 1950. King George VI, Queen Elizabeth and Princess Margaret attended, and watched the racing from the Royal Box. All the drivers in the Grand Prix and in the supporting Formula 3 race had to line up to be formally presented to the royal party. This is me bowing respectfully to His Majesty. On my left is Peter Collins, who was 18 then and starting out in Formula 3, and on my right is Wing-Commander Frank Aikens. Having won my heat, I did all I could to get past Aikens' Iota-Triumph – one of the few non-Coopers that was quick – until I burned my piston on the final corner and coasted over the line in second place. Peter just failed to catch me on the line.

We all watched the Grand Prix, which was won by Giuseppe Farina's Tipo 159 Alfa Romeo. Farina's relaxed stance in the cockpit, arms stretched out to the steering wheel, made a great impression on me and I resolved to copy it.
📷 *LAT*

➡ Between 1950 and 1954 I must have done dozens of Formula 3 races at Brands Hatch, which originally ran in an anti-clockwise direction before it was extended up to the new Druids Corner. This September 1950 shot shows me on my 21st birthday in my Mk IV Cooper, having flown back from Belfast that morning after winning the Tourist Trophy at Dundrod the day before. By now I had access to a Norton engine, and I won my heat pretty easily. In the final I spoiled my birthday by changing down from top into bottom, instead of third, and destroyed my gearbox. But the commentator started a chorus of *Twenty-One Today* and the crowd joined in, which was nice.
📷 *Guy Griffiths Collection*

➔ My first exposure to the glamour of Monte Carlo was in 1950, when there was a Formula 3 event in two heats and a final to support the Monaco Grand Prix. I found the atmosphere of the place, the people and the whole race weekend intoxicating. Over the next decade I was to become very fond of that round-the-houses track. After I had complained to JAP that my engine was down on power they flew out their latest version and we worked all night before the race to install it. But to my dismay it proved to be 1000 revs down. Even so I managed to win my heat, and here I am on the grid before the start of the final. I had to corner on the limit everywhere to make up for my lack of power, but I managed to stay ahead of Harry Schell to win. I now wore a white Herbert Johnson helmet, which cost five guineas. I wore a helmet like that for the rest of my career.

 *Stirling Moss collection*

← The Kieft that I started racing in Formula 3 in 1951 was a brilliant car, and a big leap forward from even the latest Coopers. Amazingly, it was built from scratch by Ray Martin in just 14 weeks, and first time out was the 1951 Whit Monday Goodwood. In my heat I had all sorts of teething troubles, but in the final everything gelled and it just ran away from everybody, winning by almost half a minute and breaking the Formula 3 lap record. This photo shows me with laurel wreath shaking hands with a delighted Ray Martin, still carrying his plug spanner. On the left is my friend and then manager Ken Gregory, who'd had to qualify the Kieft in Saturday practice because I was racing for HWM at Monza.
📷 *Guy Griffiths Collection*

⬇ The start of the Brands Hatch Championship final in October 1951. Pole position is on the left for the anti-clockwise circuit; on the right of my Kieft is Don Gray's Cooper. I managed to lap the entire field except for Don's brother Norman Gray, who finished second after Don retired.
📷 *Stirling Moss collection*

⬆ I was always happy to muck in with any work that needed to be done on the Kieft in the paddock. Here I am in the back of the van at the Goodwood Easter meeting in 1952: I think I'm changing the final drive chain sprocket to alter the gear ratio. It must have done the trick, because I won the race and broke the Formula 3 lap record.

📷 *Getty Images*

⬅ Brands Hatch yet again, and a fine shot from the inside of Clearways showing the distinctive forward seating position of the Kieft. It had been built around me, so I got my favoured long-arm driving position. The front/rear weight distribution with driver aboard was almost exactly 50/50, and it had adjustable suspension by rubber strands. The handling was far more stable than with a Cooper, which slid more easily although it was easy to correct. But at this event, after easily winning my heat and breaking the lap record, the Norton's con-rod broke in the final.

📷 *LAT*

⬆ Rubbing shoulders with the Grand Prix greats at the end of the 1953 British Grand Prix meeting at Silverstone. I had some dramas in the F3 race, because my clutch went on lap 3 and I had to do the remaining 12 laps stuck in fourth gear. But I still came home 16 seconds ahead of Eric Brandon. Our race was first on the programme, so after winning that I had time to get clean and changed before the prize-giving. On my immediate right is Reg Parnell, who has also changed after winning the sports car race in his works Aston Martin DB3S, and Giuseppe Farina, who won the *formule libre* race in Tony Vandervell's Thin Wall Special Ferrari. On my left is the great Alberto Ascari, who won the Grand Prix in his works Ferrari and was already on his way to his second World Championship title, and Ken Wharton, who seems to have the biggest trophy of all for finishing eighth in the Grand Prix in his Cooper-Bristol – because he was first Briton home.
📷 *LAT*

➡ For the Formula 2 race at Castle Combe that October I fitted my Cooper with its 1100cc twin-cylinder Norton engine, and among the heavier, less nimble Connaughts and Cooper-Bristols it was very competitive. On lap 2 as I braked for Quarry Corner and took my line, Tony Rolt, who was right on my tail in Rob Walker's Connaught, could not slow in time and his left front wheel struck my right rear. At once the little Cooper rolled over on me, and then carried on to finish up on its wheels on the verge. As I scrambled to my feet and made my escape Tony, still fighting for control, came across the grass after me. Fortunately he didn't catch me before I crumpled in a heap with a broken shoulder, twisted knee and various other wrenches and bruises. I was taken to hospital in Bristol but I was up and about a couple of days later. I had a bit of time to heal as my next competitive drive, in the Monte Carlo Rally, wasn't for another three months.
📷 *LAT & Stirling Moss collection*

⬆ Here I am squeezed aboard something even smaller than a 500cc Formula 3 car. This was at a masked ball held by the Enfield Arts Circle, where I had the job of judging the costumes.

📷 *Getty Images*

⬅ My final Formula 3 car was a Mk VIIA Cooper-Norton that was radically modified by Francis Beart, with all-tubular chassis, engine moved forward for better weight distribution, and a lower driving position. It was also very light. This was my first race with it, at the 1954 Easter Monday Goodwood, where I came nowhere after the engine went sick. But in the remaining nine races I did with the car I had six wins and three second places.

📷 *Ferret Fotographics*

← This picture records the end of an era for me: I'm taking the chequered flag at the end of my very last Formula 3 race, in front of the crowded stands at Aintree in October 1954.
📷 *LAT*

CHAPTER 3
THE FORMULA 2 CARS, AND THE V16 BRM

Until the beginning of 1950 all I'd done was raced the little Coopers, and I was longing to show what I could do in something bigger. Back then the single-seater staircase was very straight-forward: Formula 3 for the 500cc cars, Formula 2 for full-size racing cars with 2-litre engines, and then the top of the tree, Formula 1, using 1½-litre supercharged or 4½-litre unsupercharged power.

My Formula 3 wins were getting me noticed, and in late 1949 I was approached by John Heath. He'd set up a three-car Formula 2 team working out of Hersham & Walton Motors, the garage he ran with George Abecassis at Walton-on-Thames. His HWM cars used a 2-litre four-cylinder Alta engine and a preselector gearbox, and his chief mechanic was a Polish guy named Alphons Kowaleski, although everybody called him Alf Francis. I didn't know it then, but Alf and I were destined to work together on and off for the rest of my career.

John Heath gave me a trial around the old airfield at Odiham and, although I bashed a hole in the sump on a landing light set in the concrete surface, it went well and he signed me to drive in 1950 for 25 per cent of the start and prize money I earned. So, less than two years after my run in my first Cooper, I was a professional Formula 2 driver! The HWMs had offset cockpits so that they could be quickly converted to sports cars by adding lights and wings, the idea being to run at Le Mans as well – until John found out that it paid no start money. The cars always had to pay their way.

In fact most of my racing that year was in Europe – because of the better start money on offer – and usually in quite important Formula 2 races that often had the words 'Grand Prix' in their titles. At the time HWM was the only serious British team taking on the Continentals. In Formula 1 there was much talk of the ambitious V16 BRM project, but

that was plagued with endless problems. So we felt we were really flying the flag. In 1950 I did 21 races for HWM, of which five were in France, five in Italy, four in Belgium and one in Switzerland.

My team-mates in the other two HWMs were initially Heath and Abecassis, but then Lance Macklin was drafted into the team. Lance was a smooth operator, and going around Europe on our days off we had lots of fun together, particularly when it came to chasing crumpet. The Swiss Rudi Fischer, the Belgian Johnny Claes and the motorbike racer Fergus Anderson also had drives with us. Although the HWMs were pretty simple and straightforward, and built without any sophisticated design facilities – for example, they used front uprights and stub axles off a Standard saloon – we punched above our weight against the Ferraris, Gordinis and the like. I retired from two races, the Rome Grand Prix and the Circuito del Garda, because a front stub axle broke. And I crashed in the Naples Grand Prix when a backmarker put me into a tree; this was the first time I'd hurt myself in a racing car.

Much better was the Bari Grand Prix, which was actually a Formula 1 race. The Alfa Romeos of Farina and Fangio finished an easy 1–2, but my little Formula 2 car beat everyone else to finish a distant third. When the Alfas lapped me Farina barged past, but then he got a bit off-line and went sideways, so I squeezed up the inside and, momentarily, got in front of him again. Fangio, who had a perfect view of this just behind us and knew all about Farina's arrogance, thought it was very funny, and when he came past he gave me a huge grin. Five years later we would be team-mates at Mercedes.

For 1951 John Heath built new HWMs, proper single-seaters this time. I won first time out at Goodwood, and

Most of my racing was abroad. HWM was the only serious British team taking on the Continentals. We were flying the flag.

I scored four more wins in the UK and Ireland. But on the Continent the HWMs were starting to be outclassed. They were quite reliable by the standards of the day, and I liked the preselector box, but they weren't very light, and their Alta engines didn't really have enough power.

However, the Monza Grand Prix in May was, I reckoned, the best race of my life so far, and it introduced me to the art of slipstreaming. I found that my bulky HWM could get a tow from the Ferraris and more or less stay with them. After two heats and 195 miles of racing I finished third behind the Ferraris of Ascari and Villoresi, and beat all of the much-fancied Gordinis.

For 1952 I knew I needed a more competitive Formula 2 drive, particularly as the old Formula 1 had fizzled out and the World Championship was now being run to Formula 2. Now I'd be able to run with the big boys! Leslie Johnson, who had bought the ERA name, got David Hodkin to design a light, stiff chassis around the Bristol engine, and a lot was expected of the ERA G-type. It was very advanced for its time – but in fact it was a washout. Of the eight races I did with it, three were World Championship Grands Prix, at Spa, Silverstone and Zandvoort, and I retired from all three. In lesser British races I managed a third, a fourth, a fifth and two more retirements. By the end of the season ERA was dead, and Johnson had sold the whole project to Bristol as the basis for their 450 racing coupés.

Still desperately keen to find a British Formula 2 car that would do the job, I did three races for Connaught, but none of those brought much joy. So for 1953 I decided to follow what we had done with our successful Formula 3 Kieft, and get John 'Autocar' Cooper and Ray Martin to devise our ideal Formula 2 car. Alf Francis had now joined me as chief mechanic. We used an Alta engine and Cooper main-frame tubes, so the car was called a Cooper-Alta, but it had coil springs all round, disc front brakes and a de Dion rear with inboard drums. It just didn't work: the chassis lacked rigidity, it handled badly, and by July we had abandoned it.

Instead we bought a standard Cooper Formula 2 chassis and dropped our Alta engine into it. First race was the German Grand Prix at the Nürburgring, where I was delighted to finish sixth. Then we did the Italian Grand Prix at Monza, and I won a couple of minor races at Crystal Palace. But the car still wasn't fast enough, and I realised I would have to put my patriotism aside and look outside Great Britain if I was to have a decent go at Formula 1.

Before I did so I had a brief skirmish with the V16 BRM. This was a fantastically complex machine – 1½ litres with 16 tiny cylinders and centrifugal supercharging. The project had been announced in a blaze of publicity back in 1948, but it didn't race until 1950, and then without success.

The famous pre-war driver Raymond Mays was behind the whole thing, and in the summer of 1951 he asked me to try it on Folkingham airfield, near BRM's Lincolnshire HQ. I found it had immense power but seemed frighteningly unstable. Mays immediately offered me a contract and, although I never actually signed it, he announced to the newspapers that I had.

I had several problematic weeks testing the BRM at Monza in the September, but I didn't get to race it until June the following year. By now the V16 could no longer run in World Championship rounds, so BRM entered two cars for Fangio and me in the *formule libre* Ulster Trophy at Dundrod. The race was an embarrassing fiasco, and a few days later I wrote to Mays and told him that I didn't want to drive for BRM again.

← The 1950 offset-cockpit HWM-Alta gave me my first works drive. The Silverstone International Trophy in August was a full-blown Formula 1 race, attracting the Alfa Romeos of Fangio and Farina. This was the day the much-heralded BRM V16, Britain's great white hope for Grand Prix supremacy, made its début – and went nowhere, breaking its transmission as the starting flag fell. In my heat there was a massive cloudburst and I couldn't see a thing, so I rushed into my pit to get a visor. Nobody would find one, so I went on my way and after this delay finished ninth. Dad found me a visor for the final and, while the Alfas took an easy 1–2 ahead of Peter Whitehead's Ferrari, I was quite pleased to finish sixth.

📷 *Klemantaski Collection*

⬇ My worst moment of 1950 came in the Formula 2 Naples Grand Prix. I won my heat, and in the final I went past Franco Cortese's Ferrari to take the lead, with Lance Macklin following me. Soon after half-distance in the two-hour race I was lapping Berardo Taraschi in his little Giaur. Just as I was going round the outside of him he lost it, and his right rear wheel clouted my front left, bursting the tyre. I was catapulted off and hit a tree, breaking my kneecap on the bottom of the dash and knocking out my front teeth on the top of it. Back in London Dad was able to use his dentistry skills to fit false front teeth, which I have to this day.

📷 *Courtesy of The Revs Institute for Automotive Research, Inc*

← Our last overseas race of 1950 was the Circuito del Garda, on a fabulous 10-mile road circuit along the shores of Lake Garda, through the surrounding villages and up into the hills. There were trees, steep drops, houses, walls and marker posts: just the sort of track I loved. I was chasing the works Ferraris of Alberto Ascari and Dorino Serafini when, not for the first time, a front stub axle – a production Standard part – broke. I slithered to a halt on the brake drum while the errant wheel bounced on ahead and knocked down somebody's garden wall. The irate resident refused to return our wheel until John Heath had agreed to pay for the damage.

📷 *Stirling Moss collection*

↙ The 1951 HWM – metallic pale green, white wheels, four stub exhausts – was a good-looking racing car. In the Dutch Grand Prix at Zandvoort, a non-championship Formula 1 race, the 4½-litre Talbot-Lagos of Louis Rosier and Philippe Etancelin made the running. But I got in among them, and when Etancelin had to stop to change a blown tyre my little Formula 2 HWM was up to second. This included a pitstop to take on 15 gallons of fuel, which Alf Francis and Frank Nagel, the HWM mechanics, sloshed in from churns in 22 seconds. Then with two laps to go the bracket holding the magneto broke. I misfired into the pits, but after a quick look Alf sent me out again. In his haste he didn't replace the bonnet, and I spluttered home third without it.

📷 *Stirling Moss collection*

⬆ Taking our little team's fight to the Ferraris was always the aim, which is why I like this shot of the 1951 San Remo Grand Prix with me sandwiched between Alberto Ascari and Dorino Serafini. Actually they're lapping me, but there's no shame in that because this was a Formula 1 race, and their big 4½-litre V12s had more than double my horsepower. After three hours – races were a proper length in those days – I finished fifth, behind three F1 Ferraris and an F1 Maserati, and ahead of other F1 Maseratis and Talbot-Lagos. Even so I wasn't very pleased with myself, because I spun twice, and once I selected second instead of fourth. I was still learning.

📷 *Getty Images*

↑ The best way to describe this grid is Irish *formule* very *libre*! It was on the Curragh circuit, a difficult and bumpy five-mile layout on public roads in County Kildare, and was simultaneously the Wakefield Trophy, a scratch race, and the O'Boyle Trophy, run to a complicated handicap. In this photo the three cars on scratch are getting away: my HWM, Joe Kelly's Grand Prix Alta and Bobbie Baird's 4CLT Maserati. My HWM team-mate Duncan Hamilton is further back, behind the Lester-MG of Pat Griffith, with a weird Irish special alongside him. On scratch I led Duncan home, with Oscar Moore's own 1950 HWM making it a Walton-on-Thames 1–2–3. I also managed to make up my handicap – giving as many as six laps to some of the field – so I won the O'Boyle too. The HWM was timed on the long straight at 121.6mph.
📷 *LAT*

→ My first-ever World Championship race, in my Formula 2 HWM against the Formula 1 cars, was the 1951 Swiss Grand Prix on the glorious and very challenging Berne circuit at Bremgarten. I finished eighth in torrential rain, despite a stone breaking my aero screen early in the race. On the fast sections the wind was getting under my visor and almost lifting me out of the cockpit, and I had to steer with one hand through the rain and hold my crash-hat down on my head with the other. Alf Francis in the pits couldn't make it out: he thought I was giving some sort of secret signal!

But this picture is of the following year's Swiss Grand Prix. By now the World Championship was for F2 cars, and we had four HWMs in the race. This group is being led by Alan Brown's Cooper-Bristol from my HWM, Toulo de Graffenried's Maserati, and the HWMs of George Abecassis and Pete Collins. I got up to third behind the works Ferraris, but then George had a dreadful accident when a wheel hub broke and he was thrown onto the track. A few minutes later Pete suffered exactly the same breakage, which so rattled John Heath that he signalled for me and Lance to come in and retire. After that all our hubs were remade.
📷 *LAT*

↑ I thought the G-type ERA, with its light and stiff Elektron chassis and various clever features, was going to be the cat's whiskers, but it was never anything of the sort. This is the start of the British Grand Prix, and the works Ferraris of Alberto Ascari and Piero Taruffi have already left. I'm getting away behind Mike Hawthorn's Cooper-Bristol and Pete Collins' HWM with, just behind me, Peter Whitehead's Ferrari and Maurice Trintignant's Gordini. With its offset seating position, the ERA is visibly bulkier than the other Formula 2 cars. My miserable race lasted less than half distance before overheating and misfiring put me out.

📷 *Guy Griffiths Collection*

↗ I had to try very hard to get results out of the G-type. Here I am fighting the car at Boreham, where there was a joint F1/F2 race of Grand Prix length. Despite a lot of work, the ERA still wasn't competitive, and I finished a distant third in the F2 class, which was won by Mike Hawthorn in his far less sophisticated, and far more effective, Cooper-Bristol. That didn't cheer me at all.

📷 *Guy Griffiths Collection*

→ Here's the HWM équipe at one of the continental races: Lance Macklin looking debonair as always, me fussing over something, my girlfriend Sally Weston and *le Patron*, John Heath.

📷 *Stirling Moss collection*

⬆ After I'd more or less given up on the ERA I had a few rides in a works Connaught, starting with the Italian Grand Prix at Monza. I was determined to out-qualify Mike's Cooper-Bristol, which I managed to do by 1.4sec, but in the race my engine broke its valvegear. Froilán González, the hefty Argentinian who was leading the Maserati team, gave Ferrari quite a shock by leading the first half of the race, but a tardy fuel stop dropped him to second place behind Alberto Ascari. Here he comes up to lap me: note that sections of the Monza track were still pavé, which gave our suspensions quite a hammering. The Connaught was a beautifully made car, but just too heavy.

📷 *BRDC Archive*

⬅ The special Cooper-Alta that Ray Martin built up for me was a huge disappointment as well. This shot of me alongside Bob Gerard at Rouen demonstrates that we had a much more modern-looking car than the ubiquitous Cooper-Bristol, with its transverse leaf springing to our coil/wishbone set-up, but ours didn't work as well. In this race a fuel leak and a gearbox problem dropped us to tenth.

📷 *LAT*

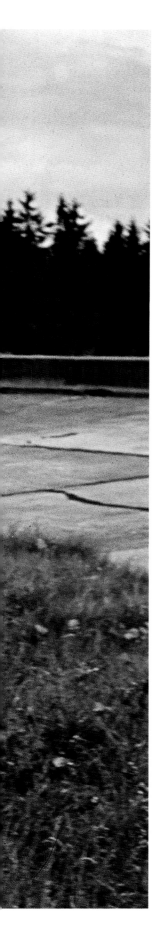

⬆ On the grid with the Cooper-Alta Special. The final indignity came in the French Grand Prix at Reims. I was flat-out going down the long straight when the flywheel exploded between my feet and came through the bell-housing, with hot bits gashing my legs like shrapnel. We gave up on it after that and switched to a conventional Cooper chassis.
📷 *Guy Griffiths Collection*

⬅ We really got the Mk II Cooper chassis as a quick fix, putting the Alta engine straight into it and setting it up to run on nitro-methane, which gave appreciably more power – at 4mpg! Alf Francis and the young lad we had to help him, Tony Robinson, put it together in 11 days and we rushed off to the Nürburgring for the German Grand Prix. I was pleased to have a decent result at last, finishing sixth behind the Ferraris and Maseratis after more than three hours around the 14-mile track.
📷 *Klemantaski Collection*

↑ While I was struggling in my efforts to stick with British cars, Mike Hawthorn had signed for Ferrari and was going very well, becoming the first Briton to win a World Championship round, at Reims in 1953. Here I'm having a quick word with him on the Zandvoort grid before the Dutch Grand Prix that year, when I had another Connaught drive. After a long pitstop with a broken fuel pipe I finished ninth; Mike had a reliable race and finished fourth.

📷 *LAT*

← The Italian Grand Prix was a race of endless drama. I got the Cooper up to fifth among the Ferraris and Masers, but then in the sweltering heat it started to throw tyre treads. I lost count of how many pitstops I had, and with four-stud wheels instead of knock-offs each tyre change took an age. Plus we sprang a fuel leak in one of the side fuel tanks, so we had to run on the tail tank and one side tank, which meant frequent refuelling. The rules allowed only two mechanics per car during the race, so I'm out of the cockpit looking after the refuelling myself. After all my delays I was determined to finish the race, which I did – nine laps behind, 13th but not last.

📷 *Getty Images*

← Instead of being Britain's world-beater, the V16 BRM was an abject failure. In 1951 I tested it briefly, and then they asked me to come to Monza for a proper development test. This photo from that test shows everybody looking surprisingly laid-back. After I'd done precisely two laps it blew one of its 16 pistons, and it took the mechanics two days to get it running again. By then I'd flown back to England to race at Goodwood, before returning to Monza for five more days. When it was going, it was very fast – I was timed at 184mph on the straight – but it gave endless trouble: overheating, another blown piston, a broken supercharger and then another engine failure. When I got home I wrote to Raymond Mays listing everything I reckoned needed fixing before it was raceworthy. It was a long letter.

📷 *Stirling Moss collection*

← For 1952 we had this smart Commer transporter, supplied by the Rootes Group. I'd been rallying for Rootes in Sunbeam-Talbots, so it was good PR for them. We provided the Cooper-Alta's measurements but the body manufacturer managed to get things wrong. When the transporter arrived Alf Francis found he couldn't shut the doors with the car inside, so he had to fit ramps to get it in at a nose-up angle. On top of all the problems we were having with the Cooper-Alta, this didn't improve his temper.

📷 *Ferret Fotographics*

⬆ I finally had a race in the V16 in June 1952, when BRM bravely entered two cars for Fangio and me in the Ulster Trophy on the treacherous Dundrod circuit. I am looking apprehensive as I get ready to go out for practice: BRM instigator Raymond Mays, with bald head, looks on, and Fangio's car is alongside. The twitchy handling, which had seemed wayward on the wide open spaces of Monza, felt positively lethal on the narrow country roads of Dundrod.

📷 *Klemantaski Collection*

⬆ Slot-racing at a show in London. On my right are Bob Gerard, in glasses, and Reg Parnell. The model cars are a BRM, a Maserati and a Ferrari: this was the only race that seemed likely to be led by a BRM.
📷 *Getty Images*

⬅ My Monza experience with the V16 should have prepared me for disaster in Ireland. At the start Fangio and I found our clutches dragging, and we both stalled. By the end of my first lap my car was overheating and the clutch was slipping, and then the gearlever knob came off in my hand. In disgust I threw it out for a spectator to keep as a souvenir. After four laps the overheating brought me in, and to my relief the car was pushed away. That was the end of me and BRM.
📷 *Klemantaski Collection*

CHAPTER 4
JOINING JAGUAR

While I was pursuing every avenue I could in single-seaters, with my sights set on Formula 1, I was also very aware of the importance of long-distance sports car racing. In 1950 I tried hard to persuade Jaguar, who had begun to campaign their beautiful XK120, that they should give me an opportunity in the classics like the Le Mans 24 Hours and the Tourist Trophy. The TT was a really demanding event, run over 320 miles of the Dundrod circuit in Northern Ireland: 7.4 miles of narrow public roads through hilly country, with fast and slow corners and a long, undulating downhill straight. I contacted Jaguar again before the TT, but word came back from team manager Lofty England that, while they accepted that I'd shown speed in Formula 3 racing, I was too inexperienced to be entrusted with one of their cars – the implication being that I would probably crash, bringing Jaguar unwelcome publicity.

Tommy Wisdom got to hear of this: he was a well-known journalist and driver, and because of his influence he'd been able to acquire one of the first production XK120s. Tommy had made a private entry for the TT, and when he heard I wanted a drive he gallantly stood down and made his car over to me; he drove a lowly Jowett Jupiter instead. Jaguar's two works cars for Peter Whitehead and Leslie Johnson were the favourites for victory, of course, and there were also works entries from Aston Martin and Allard.

I'd never been to Dundrod before, but I loved the challenging circuit, and I managed to get pole for the Le Mans-type start. This involves lining the cars up in echelon in front of the pits. The drivers stand at the other side of the road, and when the flag falls they sprint across, jump in and get going. The idea is to prove that each car has a proper self-starter.

On race day the weather was appalling: relentless rain, a gale blowing down marquees, and the spectator areas a sea of mud. Because there was a big field of cars in each class, down to the little MGs and HRGs, lapping the traffic in the spray on the narrow road was quite hairy at times. The race lasted three hours. I took the lead on lap 2, and by the end I was over three miles ahead of the works Jaguars. That made a point to Lofty England, so it was a very important victory for me. At the post-race party that night Bill Lyons, the autocratic Jaguar boss, sat me down and got my signature on a works contract for the following year. They had exciting plans to produce a competition version of the XK, the XK120C – soon abbreviated to C-type.

In 1951 I was still in an XK120 for my first experience of the Mille Miglia, with Frank Rainbow of Jaguar as my passenger. I only lasted 20 minutes before I skated off the road in the rain on oil dropped by a baby Fiat. A week later my XK won the sports car race at the big Silverstone meeting, and then I was at the Le Mans 24 Hours for the first time in one of the three new Jaguar C-types.

My job from the start was to be the pacemaker, to try to break the Ferraris and Talbot-Lagos, and when I handed over to my co-driver Jack Fairman after my first three-and-a-half-hour stint we led the Fangio/González Talbot by a full lap. We went on to lead the race for eight hours, but then in the middle of the night the oil pressure needle suddenly fell to zero, and at once the engine blew up, leaving me with a long walk back to the pits in the rain and darkness. I was not a happy bunny, although I did have the consolation of setting a new lap record.

But I was a happy bunny after the TT, which I won again, leading from start to finish. The following May came the Mille Miglia again, and with me in the C-type was Jaguar test driver and stalwart Norman Dewis. We went well until, with less than two hours to run, I slid off and broke the steering.

Word came back from Jaguar that I was too inexperienced to be entrusted with one of their cars, implying I would probably crash.

For Le Mans in 1952, in search of extra straight-line speed, Jaguar fitted longer noses to the C-types. But this made the cars overheat, and all three retired. Meanwhile my TT benefactor, Tommy Wisdom, now had a C-type of his own, and two weeks after the Le Mans fiasco he let me borrow it for a 230-mile sports car race at Reims. I persuaded Jaguar to fit to it with the Dunlop disc brakes they'd been experimenting with, and in sweltering heat I scored the first disc-braked race win in history.

All this time the C-types were also being run in British races, and I scored wins at Goodwood, Silverstone, Boreham and Turnberry. But in Britain's longest race, the Goodwood Nine Hours, Jaguar were defeated by Aston Martin. After seven hours my car, co-driven by Peter Walker, was first, and the Tony Rolt/Duncan Hamilton C-type was second. Then Tony broke a half-shaft, losing the attached wheel, and soon after Peter brought our car in with a broken arm in the rear suspension. The two mechanics allocated to our car replaced the arm in 32 minutes, and I rejoined to take a distant fifth place.

For Le Mans in 1953 Jaguar built lighter C-types with disc brakes, which gave us a great advantage, particularly at the end of the Mulsanne Straight, over the very strong entry of Ferraris, Lancias, Alfas, Gordinis, Talbots and Astons. I led from the start, but during the second hour my car developed a misfire. It took two lengthy stops to trace and replace a blocked fuel filter, and I rejoined at the tail of the field. After 18 hours Peter Walker and I had worked our way back up to second place, by which time the Rolt/Hamilton C-type was four laps ahead, so we dutifully followed them home for a Jaguar 1–2.

The Reims race was now run over 12 hours, starting at midnight and finishing at noon, three hours before the start of the French Grand Prix. Peter Whitehead and I won with our C-type and then I switched to the Cooper-Alta for the Formula 1 race. At Dundrod I failed to make it three TT wins in a row when my back axle broke three laps from the end, and we were beaten by the Astons again in the Goodwood Nine Hours. Walker and I led from the start until, with one hour to go, the engine threw a rod.

Jaguar's revolutionary new D-type made its début in the 1954 Le Mans 24 Hours, but Peter Walker and I retired during the night with brake problems. Le Mans was never a lucky race for me. My three races in a D-type all ended in retirement: at Reims a drive shaft broke, and in the TT a piston failed. That's why I look back on the C-type with much more affection – and, while the D had been much faster than the C on the wide open spaces of Le Mans, it felt less at home around Dundrod.

When I wasn't busy for Jaguar, I was offered lots of other sports car drives. Most of these cars are shown on the following pages. Two that I remember fondly are Syd Greene's Frazer-Nash Le Mans Replica, which I used to win the British Empire Trophy on the Isle of Man, and Briggs Cunningham's little Osca MT4, which I shared with Bill Lloyd to win the 1954 Sebring 12 Hours.

I was back at Sebring the following year to share an Austin-Healey 100S with Lance Macklin. The four-pot Austin engine had been used in taxis and vans, so it didn't rev much, although it had good torque. Lance and I did the 12 Hours with no bother, and our humble Healey finished a very pleasing sixth overall behind Ferraris and Maseratis and the winning D-type. I did one of my better Le Mans starts that day: I was 33rd in the line-up and over the start line I was delighted to be in second place!

➜ This was my first works Jaguar drive, in a more or less standard XK120 in the sports car race at the Silverstone International Trophy meeting on 5 May 1951. The XK handled so well that I found I could take Silverstone's long, open corners in a series of tyre-howling drifts, and I was so far in front by the end of the one-hour race that I eased off, but still came home almost a minute and a half ahead of four more XK120s. Here I've just lapped Sydney Allard's J2 Allard.

📷 *Klemantaski Collection*

⬇ The Moss équipe after my Silverstone win: Mum and Dad, with pipe, flanking my girlfriend Sally Weston. There were constant rumours that Sally and I were engaged, but we never were. After I told a journalist that, a headline in the *Daily Mail* read: 'Just Friends Says Car Ace'.

📷 *Guy Griffiths Collection*

⬆ My win in the 1950 Tourist Trophy, the day before my 21st birthday, represented a milestone in my career. Jaguar had refused me a works drive, citing my inexperience, so I raced Tommy Wisdom's XK120 and beat the works cars hands down. The weather was dreadful throughout, and the narrow Dundrod circuit, seven or more miles of country public roads, was treacherously slippery. I'd never raced an XK120 before, but it handled superbly and despite the conditions I quickly felt happy with it and really enjoyed the drive. This shot shows me going through a fast left-hander in front of a bedraggled group of hardy spectators, who can't have been happy when the high winds blew down the beer tent. At the post-race party Jaguar acknowledged they'd misjudged me by getting my signature on a contract for 1951.

📷 *LAT*

⬆ The Tourist Trophy turned out to be a lucky race for me, just as Le Mans turned out to be an unlucky one. I did the TT nine times, and won seven; I did Le Mans ten times, and never won it. Here I am wearing the laurel wreath after winning the 1951 TT in the C-type, having led from start to finish. At least it was dry that year, but I wasn't taking any risks with the Irish weather: instead of racing overalls, I'm wearing an anorak and a sweater.

📷 *LAT*

← At the start of the 1952 Mille Miglia with Norman Dewis, I upset the organisers by refusing to drive onto the starting ramp because I had an idea it might clout something vital on the C-type's underside. The car on the ramp is the Biondetti Jaguar Special, which started one minute behind us. We kept going for 850 of the 1000 miles, even though we had all the usual Mille Miglia dramas. The C-type took a terrible pounding on the rough Italian roads: a tyre threw a tread and we had to change the wheel on the verge, soon the rear shockers were shot, and we developed a fuel leak. Nevertheless, we were on target for fourth place at least when, coming down the Raticosa Pass with less than 150 miles to go, I understeered off into a rock, breaking the steering. Very disappointing.
📷 *BRDC Archive*

↓ Expensive scrapyard! The 1952 Monaco Grand Prix was run for sports cars, over 100 laps. My C-type led until almost half-distance, when Robert Manzon's very quick Gordini passed me. Just then, as Reg Parnell was negotiating Ste Devote, the engine of his Aston Martin DB3 blew up spectacularly, covering the road with oil. Antonio Stagnoli's Ferrari crashed into the Aston, and then Manzon and I arrived. There was no adhesion whatever, and we both piled into the Aston, and so did Tony Hume's Allard. Two British spectators hopped over the barriers and helped me pull crumpled bodywork off the C-type's wheels, and I managed to drive it back to the pits where the Jaguar mechanics did the job properly and got me back into the race, which was now led by a string of Ferraris. I managed to climb back to fifth place. But after I'd done my best to put on a decent show, the race organisers chose to black-flag me and disqualify me for receiving outside assistance.
📷 *Stirling Moss collection*

⬇ For the 1952 Le Mans, Jaguar made a rare mistake. After the Mille Miglia I sent Bill Lyons a telegram telling him we needed more straight-line speed to beat the Italians. So hasty modifications were made to the C-type, with a longer, lower nose and an extended tail. But there was no time to test the changes, and as soon as practice began we realised the cars were overheating. The header tank had been moved, and apparently the water was bypassing the radiator and just circulating straight back into the engine. Frantically, extra vents were cut in the body sides, but in the race all three team cars were early retirements. Mine lasted just 24 laps before it retired, not from overheating but because oil starvation ran the bearings after a relief valve jammed. The photo shows the start just after we've run across the road and leaped into our cars. I'm in C-type No 17 and Tony Rolt is in C-type No 18, neck and neck with Pierre Levegh's Talbot No 8 – which he drove single-handed, and so nearly won the race – and Sidney Allard's Allard No 4.

📷 *Stirling Moss collection*

⬆ A great shot of the traditional Le Mans start, taken as the flag fell for the sports car race at the 1952 Silverstone May International. I'm nearest the camera. As a runner at school I used to manage the 100 yards in 10 seconds, so I always tried to get an advantage on these occasions, even to getting down on one knee in a sprinter's crouch. There were three works C-types entered for me, Peter Walker and Tony Rolt. Peter and Tony both ran into problems, but I had a clear run to win ahead of the DB3 Aston Martins of Reg Parnell and George Abecassis.

A few strange things happened in Le Mans starts. There was the time somebody jumped into the wrong car, and on another occasion Tony Rolt put his foot through the steering wheel. To annoy me, Mike Hawthorn once started running across before the flag had fallen. I shouted after him: 'You bastard, Hawthorn!' Whereupon he collapsed on the track in fits of giggles.

📷 *Guy Griffiths Collection*

⬆ Another true road race: the British Empire Trophy in the Isle of Man. I'd won it in 1951 with a little Frazer-Nash but the course was a bit tight and twisty for the C-type, and was better suited to the more nimble Aston Martin DB3Ss, so I could only finish fourth in the 1953 race. Here I am being followed through Parkfield Bend by the Ecurie Ecosse C-type of Jimmy Stewart, whose kid brother Jackie was later to do quite well in motor racing.
📷 *Stirling Moss collection*

⬅ I'm talking here to Jaguar boss Bill (later Sir William) Lyons, who was a great believer in racing's power to boost the reputation of his normal production cars, and used to come to a lot of the races. I had taken to wearing a body belt to support my stomach and abdominal muscles, because – long before the days of seat belts – you could take quite a battering in the cockpit being thrown about by the cornering forces.
📷 *LAT*

⬆ I was destined not to get a third TT victory at Dundrod in 1953. Peter
Walker and I were in the lead for most of the race in our C-type, but in the
closing laps it developed the same gearbox problem that had already put
out the Rolt/Hamilton sister car. I struggled on, and three laps from the end
I stopped just before the finish line and waited for the race to end. When
Peter Collins took the flag in the winning Aston Martin DB3S I gave him a
wave, and then restarted the Jaguar and was just able to chug over the line
to classify us fourth overall, and winner of the over 3-litre class.
📷 *LAT*

⬆ This shot clearly demonstrates the variety that used to run at Le Mans in the 1950s, with my Jaguar D-type passing a little Renault saloon, chased by one of the centre-seat Gordinis. The 1954 race gave me my first taste of the ultra-streamlined D, with its Malcolm Sayer-created aerodynamics and tail fin at Le Mans for extra straight-line stability. While Rolt/Hamilton battled magnificently to the end with the González/Trintignant Ferrari and only just lost, Peter Walker and I were delayed early on by a blocked fuel filter (for the second year running). After that we were catching up well when, at around 1am, I arrived at the end of the Mulsanne Straight, doing over 170mph, to find my brakes had failed completely and the pedal went to the floor. Fortunately I was able to use the main N138 to Tours as an escape road, do a U-turn and return to the pits to retire.

📷 *Stirling Moss collection*

← A great shot of my D-type accelerating out of the Dundrod hairpin, its nose peppered with the scars of flying stones from the loose tarmac, during the 1954 Tourist Trophy. The post-war TT had so far always been a handicap event, although the fastest cars were usually able to overcome their handicap during the race, so that the final order at the front tended to be the same as the scratch order. But for the 1954 TT the handicaps were much more severe, based on engine size, so Lofty England decided to have short-stroke 2.4-litre engines built up for two of the three D-types entered. Peter Walker and I shared one of these, and of course it was slower that the 3.4 version, but we were running well and likely to finish in the top three on handicap when a piston failed with less than an hour to go. Just like the previous year I stopped in front of the line to await the finish. I spent so long stationary that we were only credited with 18th place. Because of the handicap the winner, bizarrely, was a 750cc twin-cylinder Panhard.

📷 *Ferret Fotographics*

⬆ The BRDC Gold Star was awarded each year on a complicated points system to the most successful British racing driver in all types of events. Between 1950 and 1961 I managed to win it 10 times, although in 1953 Mike Hawthorn pipped me because of his French Grand Prix win, and we tied in 1958. Here I am being presented with the gong in 1952 by Prince Philip, Duke of Edinburgh, at the Royal Festival Hall for the BRDC's 25th anniversary dinner, a grand white-tie-and-tails affair; he was President-in-Chief of the club at the time. It all went on until 3am, and while the names on the cabaret list won't mean much today, they were glittering then: Peter Ustinov, Jimmy Edwards and Billy Cotton, and Edmundo Ros and his Rumba Band.

📷 *Stirling Moss collection*

⬅ The Frazer-Nash Le Mans Replica, with its 2-litre Bristol engine, was like an offset Formula 2 car with wings, and it handled well and was great to drive once you got used to the very high-geared steering. The British Empire Trophy was a two-hour race around a 3.8-mile circuit on the Isle of Man, through the streets and surrounding roads of Douglas, and Syd Greene, a great enthusiast who was denied a race licence because he had lost an arm, asked me to drive his 'Nash in the 1951 event. It was another handicap race and I had to give three credit laps to the rapid Lester-MG of Pat Griffith, which was still ahead of me when it ran out of oil and seized with two laps to go. Rotten luck for Pat and good luck for me, because I wouldn't have caught him.

📷 *LAT*

The trophy inscription reads (partially legible):

THE R.I.R. NISUMSSR TROPHY
AWARDED
TO THE
INDEX OF PERFORMANCE
WINNER OF THE
1954
INTERNATIONAL
12 HOUR GRAND PRIX OF ENDURANCE
SEBRING, FLORIDA
MARCH 7, 1954

⬆ This is the little 1450cc Osca MT4 that won the 1954 Sebring 12 Hours. I'd met that great American sportsman Briggs Cunningham at Le Mans, where he fielded his eponymous cars each year, and in March 1954 he asked me to drive his Osca at Sebring, sharing with his wife's cousin Bill Lloyd. I had never been to America before, and I jumped at the chance. I didn't think our little car had much hope of victory against the works Ferraris, Lancias and Aston Martins, but it turned out to handle beautifully, and for its size it was quick. The Lancias, with drivers like Fangio, Ascari, Villoresi and Castellotti, were the early leaders but one by one they fell by the wayside, and so did the Ferraris and Astons, and we were left out in front ahead of the sole-surviving Lancia. The Osca never missed a beat for the whole 12 hours, although for at least half the race its brakes were completely gone. But on the wide open runways of Sebring Bill and I became adept at slowing it down for corners by chucking it sideways.

📷 *Ozzie Lyons/www.petelyons.com*

⬅ Surprised and delighted, Bill and I celebrate our Sebring victory. I smoked a bit in those days, and a tobacco company paid me the huge sum of £500 to appear in an ad saying: 'I don't smoke often, but when I do I'm choosy. I smoke Craven A.' However, I wouldn't have been able to enjoy that bottle of Moët et Chandon: in those days I never drank alcohol.

📷 *LAT*

⬆ This Lister-Bristol was usually driven by Archie Scott Brown, who had some great battles in 2-litre sports car races with Roy Salvadori's A6GCS Maserati. Its creator Brian Lister asked me to drive it at Goodwood in September 1954, and I too found myself fighting Roy's Maserati. This picture must have been taken in practice, because we raced nose to tail for the whole race, but I never found a way past and finished second, 0.6sec behind him, although I did have the consolation of setting fastest lap.
📷 *LAT*

⬅ This is a Leonard-MG, built up by Lionel Leonard on his own chassis, which was very much like the twin-tube, transverse-leaf Cooper layout. The shapely aluminium body style, copied from the *barchetta* Ferrari of the day, was also used by Cliff Davis for his Cooper-MG and then his Tojeiro-Bristol, which went on to become the prototype of the AC Ace. In 1954 Lionel asked me to drive his car in the British Empire Trophy, which had now moved from the Isle of Man to Oulton Park. I finished third in my heat and was lying second in class in the final when the crank broke.
📷 *LAT*

⬆ With its flared front wheel arches the Connaught ALSR looked like a mini-Aston Martin DB3S. This car belonged to Peter Bell, and I drove it for him at Montlhéry, France, and Oulton Park. Although it was a bit big and heavy for a 1500cc car, it handled well and I won my class both times. The race at Oulton was a big 220-mile international, and I finished seventh overall and first small car home behind the works Aston Martins and Ferraris.
📷 *LAT*

⬅ The 500cc Formula 3 was coming to the end of its days when I was racing the Francis Beart-modified Cooper in 1954, so Beart decided to move up into the 1100cc sports-racing car class, which was gaining popularity thanks to the effectiveness of the little single-cam Coventry Climax engine. Bernie Rodger built the car for Beart and, although it had a very shapely body, it was fairly conventional underneath. I only raced it twice. It was barely finished for the 1955 Easter Monday Goodwood, still unpainted, and didn't handle very well, but after three laps I was leading the class when the throttle cable broke. Four weeks later I ran it at Silverstone, painted now, but the ignition played up and the driver's door fell open. It was all a bit of a contrast from everything else going on in my life: the week before I'd been winning the Mille Miglia, that day I was racing my own Maserati 250F, and two weeks later I was leading the Monaco Grand Prix for Mercedes. I don't know what happened to the Beart-Climax after that.
📷 *Klemantaski Collection*

↑ The Nassau Speed Week in December each year, run around the local Windsor airfield, was always a good way to escape the English winter, with lots of sociable parties. In 1955 I got to drive an Austin-Healey 100S. I finished sixth behind the Ferraris and Maseratis in the Governor's Cup, and then retired from the Nassau Trophy when, as shown, my front suspension collapsed, puncturing a tyre.

📷 *Stirling Moss collection*

➜ During my 1955 Mercedes season I got the chance to race another German car when the team gave the Goodwood Nine Hours a miss. Porsche approached me to drive one of their Type 550 1500cc Spyders, sharing with Huschke von Hanstein, who is chatting to me with camera round his neck as the cars are lined up for the Le Mans-type start. The car was very quick, and with 90 minutes left we were racing on through the darkness, leading our class by six laps and running sixth overall. Then Tony Crook's Cooper-Bristol blew up right in front of me at Woodcote. Tony spun on own his oil and I couldn't avoid him and hit him amidships, crunching my front suspension.

I also drove works Porsches as far apart as Portugal and New Zealand, winning each time, and my other 550 drive was in the lighter spaceframe car in the 1958 Buenos Aires 1000Kms, the first round of the World Sports Car Championship. Jean Behra and I rather annoyed the Ferrari team by finishing third overall on the same lap as the winning Ferrari Testa Rossa, winning our class by seven laps. A really great little car.

📷 *National Motor Museum/MPL*

↑ In small sports car racing in the mid-1950s the battles were always between the rear-engined, centre-seat Cooper, with its sawn-off 'bob-tail' rear end, and the Lotus 11, with its Frank Costin-styled aerodynamic shape. The start of the 1500cc heat at the 1956 British Empire Trophy at Oulton Park showed the rivalry, with my Cooper, Mike Hawthorn's Lotus, Roy Salvadori's Cooper and Colin Chapman's Lotus filling the front row. I only managed fourth in the heat, but in the final the little cars were much quicker around the twisty Oulton track than the Aston DB3Ss and the D-types, and the battle for the lead was between my Cooper and Chapman's Lotus. I led, then the Lotus boss passed me, then he had a quick spin. Thereafter I had the race in the bag, coming home 10 seconds ahead of the recovering Chapman, Salvadori and Hawthorn – so it was Cooper, Lotus, Cooper, Lotus.

🖒 LAT

→ My sister Pat, already well-known as a top British show-jumper, had done some rallying with her own Triumph TR2 and gone really well. So in 1955 she tried to persuade Triumph to pay some of her expenses to do the biggest British event of the day, the RAC Rally. They refused, so she went to MG who offered to loan a TF sports car and pay expenses. Here she is showing me the car. Triumph must have kicked themselves later, for within five years, as a works BMC driver, she was Women's Rally Champion and won the Liège-Rome-Liège outright in a big Healey. Soon after that she won the Tulip Rally outright, this time in a Mini-Cooper.

🖒 Getty Images

CHAPTER 5
RALLYING AND RECORDS, AND FUN IN SALOONS

During the early 1950s, when each year's European season came to an end, there was no racing during the winter – which meant I wasn't earning anything. This was before the Tasman series started to attract drivers from the Northern Hemisphere, and before the top events in South America became truly international. All through my career I always believed that, as a professional racer, I needed to spend every possible moment racing.

Today's Grand Prix star will do nothing outside Formula 1. He'll just take part in the 20 or so rounds a year and, as testing is now limited by the regulations, I suppose he spends the rest of the year being nice to his sponsors and working out in the gym. I didn't go to the gym. I kept fit by working out in as many cockpits as I could get into. I would do up to 80 races a year in every sort of category – more if you counted rallying and record-breaking, and having a go in anything else that presented itself, from a mud-plugging trial to the London-to-Brighton veteran car run.

Apart from a couple of light-hearted attempts, one with Lance Macklin in a borrowed Aston Martin DB2 and one in a friend's Morris Minor, I'd never really considered that specialised category of motor sport known as rallying. But in late 1951 Norman Garrad, a friendly chap who was the sales boss of the Rootes group and also ran their competition side, asked me to join their team for the Monte Carlo Rally. On offer was a fee of £50, and it sounded like fun, so of course I said 'yes'.

In those days the thriving British motor industry consisted of the Big Five: Ford, BMC, Vauxhall, Standard-Triumph and Rootes. Most of all that has disappeared now, more's the pity. Rootes was run by the tough, energetic Billy Rootes, later Lord Rootes, and his brother Reggie, and their portfolio included Hillman, Humber, Sunbeam-Talbot and later Singer, as well as truck manufacturers Commer and Karrier. Norman wanted to promote the Sunbeam-Talbot 90, their sportiest saloon, in rallying. In those days 'the Monte', run every year in January when the weather was at its worst, was the most prestigious rally, with starting points as far apart as Glasgow and Warsaw and converging on Monaco before the decisive final section through the French Alps.

On that first Monte, in 1952, I took John '*Autocar*' Cooper and BRDC secretary Desmond Scannell with me. That year the weather was dreadful and the roads were very difficult, but we got to Monte Carlo without penalty. Then came the final mountain test, and in the end we very nearly won the thing. You had to be precise on their timings to the second, and our Sunbeam and Sydney Allard's big Allard saloon were both early at the finish, but by less than half a minute. We lost out because we were 4sec earlier than him! That second place put me very much in Rootes' good books, and later that year I did the other really gruelling European event, the Alpine Rally. In 1953 it was the Monte again: the weather was much milder, so many more crews got to Monaco unpenalised, and it wasn't nearly so much fun. We finished sixth.

In the Alpine Rally you were given a Coupe des Alpes if you could finish the whole thing without penalty. And if you could do that three years running you received a Coupe d'Or – a Gold Cup. Up to then only one man, Ian Appleyard with his Jaguar XK120, had ever done that. On the 1952 Alpine I managed to finish with no penalties, so that was a Coupe. In 1953 Rootes introduced a new open two-seater version of the 90 saloon called, appropriately, the Sunbeam Alpine, and that year I finished without penalty again. So for 1954 I really wanted to do the event again – and go for a Gold.

Even though the Alpine Rally was run in July, that year up in the mountains it might as well have been January, with some of the passes blocked by drifting snow. The gearbox wasn't up

I didn't go to the gym. I kept fit by working out in as many cockpits as I could, doing up to 80 races a year.

to the constant punishment, from bottom-gear hairpins to overdrive top on the few straight sections, and soon we had lost first and fourth gears, although overdrive on the remaining gears helped. The final section from Cortina to Cannes was incredibly demanding. Coming down from the mountains I had to drive absolutely flat out for kilometre after kilometre, and even so we only just made the control within our time by a split second. After three days on the limit in extremely difficult conditions we were still without penalty, and the release of tension was such that I did something I've never done before or since in my racing career – I burst into tears!

But there was one remaining hurdle. In post-rally scrutineering you had to prove that everything on your car was still working. A rival – we never found out who – tipped off the officials about our gearbox problem, and I had to take a scrutineer up the road to prove that I still had four gears. I started off in second, saying 'Voilà, première!', and then waggled the gear lever while I unobtrusively flicked the overdrive switch: 'Voilà, deuxième!' Then I changed into third while flicking back to direct drive, then waggled the gear lever again while switching into overdrive third: "Voilà, quatrième!" The official was satisfied, and we were clear. It's the only time in my career I can ever remember cheating. But after what we'd been through, we bloody well deserved our Coupe d'Or.

Record-breaking – setting maximum speed marks in various classes over measured distances – was a popular promotional tool in those days, and even if you weren't actually breaking a class record the speed you achieved, if it sounded high enough, would still be used in publicity. I did over 120mph in a Sunbeam Alpine along the Jabbeke motorway in Belgium, a popular venue for this sort of thing, and in a Humber Super Snipe four of us managed to visit 15 European countries in four days.

I also set some records at Monza with an all-enclosed Lotus 11, until it broke. But the most memorable record-breaking I did was for MG. They produced an extraordinary and very clever projectile of only 1500cc for me to drive on the Bonneville Salt Flats in the USA. With the help of a supercharger I managed over 245mph, and the car clocked up five new world records in its class.

I set some speed targets for Jaguar too, notably when Leslie Johnson and I averaged over 100mph for 24 hours in an XK120 roadster at Montlhéry in 1950. We went back in 1952 with a coupé XK120 and managed 100mph for a week. And that same year Jaguar introduced me to saloon car racing, which was a comparatively new idea then.

Jaguar's big and bulky four-door Mk VII, using the same engine as the XK120, had the highest performance of any car of its type in the world, and Bill Lyons was keen to demonstrate that fact. I raced the Mk VII three years running at the Silverstone International Trophy meeting, and won in 1952 and '53. In '54, going for the hat-trick, I ran across the road in the Le Mans-type start and jumped in – and the starter motor jammed. When I finally got going everybody else was long gone, but I managed to come through the traffic and finish third, sitting behind the other two works Mk VIIs of Ian Appleyard and Tony Rolt.

At the lower end of the horsepower spectrum, I raced a more or less unmodified Standard 10 at Oulton Park in 1955. It was no great shakes, but it was familiar to me because my short-distance road car then was a much-modified Standard 8. Other very different vehicles that I got my backside into during the winter months included a trials special, a 1903 Cadillac in the London-to-Brighton veteran car run, and, when I was in Australia in 1956, the locally-built WM Special. Variety, they say, is the spice of life.

← This was my first serious rally, the Monte Carlo in 1952. The picture shows us on the descent back into Monaco, with the roads dry for a change, but where it mattered the weather was really severe that year, with deep snow and black ice. Out of several hundred starters, we were one of only 15 crews to reach Monte Carlo without penalty – and then came the crucial last mountain section. At one point I slid nose-first into a snowdrift, but John Cooper, Desmond Scannell and I were able to manhandle the car back onto the road and carry on. But our lack of rally experience meant we had forgotten to take note of how long we had been stationary. As I rushed back down towards the finish all three of us made different estimates, so we calculated the average between the three of us and John counted me off to the finish on his stopwatch. We weren't far off: the timekeepers decreed that we'd arrived 28 seconds early. Sydney Allard's big Allard saloon was 24 seconds early. So, at our first attempt, we had lost the rally by 4 seconds. Norman Garrad of Rootes was delighted with our second place, and our class win, and more rides for Sunbeam-Talbot followed.

📷 *Stirling Moss collection*

← When we got back to London we found that Sydney's winning drive wasn't the only one that had made headlines, as we were getting plaudits as well. The BBC summoned us to Broadcasting House for a radio interview with the top motoring broadcaster, Raymond Baxter. With him here in the studio are John Cooper (left) and me.

📷 *Stirling Moss collection*

⬆ John Cooper, Desmond Scannell and I did the Monte again in 1953 and the weather was better, but it was still cold. I am wearing what I suppose would now be called a 'onesie', padded and waterproof, and a bobble hat. Very fetching. John wore a sports anorak and beret. Des, typically, tackled the rally wearing a double-breasted suit, with breast-pocket handkerchief and polished black shoes; a scarf was his only concession to the temperature. Note the car's rally trim: hoods over three auxiliary lights to reduce glare in driving snow, Perspex snow deflector on the bonnet, old-fashioned bar heater on the driver's side of the windscreen, and roof rack carrying spare tyres. We finished sixth.

📷 *Getty Images*

↑ Despite the open sunroof, there's no time for my navigator John Cutts and me to admire the glorious scenery on the 1952 Alpine Rally as our Sunbeam-Talbot 90 storms up a loose gravel track over one of the lesser-known mountain passes. In a 2000-mile route we had to climb more than 40 of these passes. At one stage our exhaust system fell off and we lost 26 minutes replacing it, but by driving on the limit for the rest of the rally we reached the end without penalties, winning a Coupe des Alpes – and the three works Sunbeam-Talbots took the team prize. Mike Hawthorn drove one of the sister entries as I'd persuaded him that the Alpine Rally was a fun way to earn £50, with the possibility of some crumpet-chasing after the finish in Cannes.

📷 *Stirling Moss collection*

→ The 1953 Alpine gave John Cutts and me our first rally in the new two-seater Sunbeam, appropriately called the Sunbeam Alpine; they'd now dropped Talbot from the name. Rootes employed some more racing drivers for this event: Peter Collins, who went out with back axle trouble, and John Fitch, who did the distance without penalty. We had our troubles – wheel nuts working loose, a plug lead coming adrift, our rally plate falling off, all of which lost us time – but we made it to the end with no penalties, so we got another Coupe. This shot shows again the loose, gravelly surface of the mountain passes we were driving on. The bonnet, secured by a strap, is deliberately open to get some more cooling air around the hard-worked engine.

📷 *LAT*

← To coincide with the Sunbeam Alpine's announcement, Rootes decided to raise the car's profile by clocking some high-speed runs. A car was carefully prepared with aero screen and rigid tonneau around the cockpit, and I managed to average 116mph around the banked Montlhéry track near Paris. Then Leslie Johnson stayed out on the circuit for an hour and travelled 111.2 miles. The day before, the Belgian police closed one carriageway of the motorway from Jabbeke to Aeltre, and after we'd pumped up the tyres to 75psi to reduce rolling resistance I was timed at 120.4mph – which, over 60 years ago in a production car with not much more than 80bhp from its four-pot engine, wasn't half bad. This is the Alpine passing the timekeepers' van at the end of the measured mile.

📷 *Stirling Moss collection*

← As another publicity stunt, Rootes decided that it should be possible to visit 15 European countries in five days. In fact we managed it in three days 18 hours. The car was a lumbering Humber Super Snipe, and our only problem was one puncture. We were four on board: Leslie Johnson and me doing the driving, John Cutts navigating, and David Humphrey as riding mechanic. We started in Oslo, and from Norway we went through Sweden, Denmark, Germany, Holland, Belgium, Luxembourg, France, Switzerland, Lichtenstein, Austria, Italy, Yugoslavia, Spain and Portugal, finishing in Lisbon. John had worked out a clever route so that for some of the countries we only had to nip across the borders and back, but it was still a distance of 3280 miles, averaging 900 miles a day. And we did it in December when the weather was truly awful, with frequent blizzards and lots of ice.

📷 *Stirling Moss collection*

OUNTRIES IN 5 DAYS OSLO TO LISBON

GB
MRW 671

⬆ Our crew poses for a quick photo in Copenhagen with, from left, David, John, Leslie and me. I'm carrying a good supply of what was then my favourite tipple.
📷 *Getty Images*

→ Colin Chapman wanted to
attack international speed records
in the 1100cc class, so a Lotus 11
was taken to Monza in September
1956, and I stayed on after I'd won
the Italian Grand Prix to drive it
around the bumpy banked bowl
the next day. Frank Costin's body
shape for the Lotus was extremely
aerodynamic, and when he
designed a Perspex bubble to
marry up with the headrest the
result was very slippery indeed.
The canopy was fixed, so I had to
worm my way into the car through
the tiny drop-down door – in this
picture Frank is holding the door
as I settle into the seat. Frank had
cleverly arranged for the canopy
to be ventilated without incurring
extra drag, with a slit below the
screen and slots behind my head
for the air to escape. Otherwise it
would have been unendurable
in there.

   I did 50kms at 135.5mph and
50 miles at 132.7mph, and I was
pressing on for 100kms and
100 miles when, thanks to the
battering of the banking, the back
of the car started to fall to pieces.
At over 130mph a frame tube
broke, the entire rear bodywork
flew off, and the battery fell into
the road and was dragged along
by its earth lead. I flew home, and
when the car was mended they
had another go, this time with the
American driver Mackay Fraser.
📷 *LAT*

↑ This is the amazing super-streamlined MG EX181 that I drove in 1957 on the baking hot, blinding white Salt Lake Flats at Bonneville, Utah. The people at MG designed the body first: the perfect shape was evolved, and then a chassis made to fit under it carrying all the components inside the shell. One of the components was the driver, who was squashed in ahead of the engine with his legs right out in front of the front wheels. The only way they could find space for the steering wheel was to mount it horizontally. Its engine was developed for the yet-unannounced MGA Twin-Cam, but with a massive Shorrock supercharger, giving an output of nearly 200bhp per litre from just 1500cc. It was so high-geared that I changed into fourth gear at over 200mph, and because of the efficient aerodynamics I needed a lot of distance to get it stopped.

📷 *Stirling Moss collection*

↗ We broke five world records in the MG's class over varying distances from one kilometre to five miles, and our best speed, as a mean in two directions to average out the effect of any wind, was 245.6mph. A black line had been painted dead straight for seven miles across that featureless white desert, and trying to keep EX181 on that line at nearly 250mph was a very different experience. In some of the publicity afterwards the record was advertised as four miles a minute or a mile in 15 seconds, which does sound quite quick.

📷 *Getty Images*

→ The bodywork had to be removed to get me in, and then fastened down on top of me. So I was totally shut in, with an inch or two to spare, and if anything had gone wrong I wouldn't have been able to get myself out.

📷 *Getty Images*

← After Jaguar had signed me as a works driver on the evening of my TT victory in 1950, my first job for them came five weeks later at Montlhéry. Leslie Johnson persuaded Bill Lyons that an XK120 could average 100mph for 24 hours, and asked to have me as his co-driver. We decided to take three hours each, and because it was late October we had 13 hours of darkness. Despite a couple of extra spot lamps, at that speed the lighting wasn't great, but we beat our target quite easily, averaging 107.4mph.

📷 *Stirling Moss collection*

⬆ When the new coupé version of the XK120 was announced, Jaguar sorted me out one of my own, painted green and cream. I asked for left-hand drive because I wanted it for fast travel on the Continent. In those days the quickest way to cross the Channel was in one of the Bristol freighters operated by Silver City Airways, which charged £19 (not so cheap then!) for the flight from Lympne to Le Touquet.

📷 *Getty Images*

⬅ In 1951 Leslie Johnson decided it should be possible to average 100mph for a week, including all necessary stops. We returned to Montlhéry with an XK120 coupé, and got Jack Fairman and Bert Hadley to help share the driving chores. At 120mph a lap of the Montlhéry banked track took less than a minute, so in a three-hour stint we would each do more than 350 laps. It required great concentration, and at the same time it could get very boring.

We relieved the boredom with various pranks. At the dead of night Leslie was horrified when his headlights picked out a ghostly figure, ten feet tall with a long cloak and a pointed hat, looming out of the darkness. In fact it was me on Jack Fairman's shoulders with a tarpaulin wrapped around me and a fuel funnel on my head. Leslie got his revenge by putting a pit board on the track opposite the timekeepers' hut, and then each lap moving the board closer and closer to the hut, so I had a narrower and narrower gap to go through.

It was a long week, but when it was done we had covered 16,851.7 miles, an average speed of 100.3mph. Perched on our car in this victory photo are (from right) Jack, me, Leslie and Bert. In the white shirt behind us is our team manager, Mort Morris-Goodall.

📷 *Stirling Moss collection*

↑ I soon had my XK coupé fitted with wire wheels, which looked much smarter, and to keep busy I did a British rally in November 1952, taking John Cooper with me again. This was the MCC *Daily Express* Rally, with road sections around the country, speed trials and then driving tests at the finish. We only came 14th, but we won our class, and then at the end there was a coachwork contest. We cleaned up the XK and put on a set of white-wall tyres – in those days they were considered quite stylish – and we won another pot. I also went to France for the Lyons-Charbonnières Rally, taking *Autosport* editor Gregor Grant as my navigator, and we got second in class.

📷 *LAT*

→ The Jaguar Mk VII looked big and unwieldy, but in fact around the wide open spaces of Silverstone it handled surprisingly well, accompanied by so much tyre squeal that people said they could hear me coming long before they could see me. With the XK engine it had straight-line speed as well. Nowadays touring cars are so carefully developed and race-prepared that they bear very little relation to cars on the production line, but Lofty England was determined that when I raced the Mk VII it should be as standard as possible – 'We race our cars as we sell them' – so nobody could complain that Jaguar were running a specially prepared car. He wouldn't even let me have a bucket seat, and of course there were no seat belts then, so to prevent myself from ending up on the passenger's side in right-hand corners I used to put my foot across to the left-hand door to brace myself. This shot shows the first time I raced the Mk VII, during the 1952 May Silverstone International meeting, understeering somewhat but actually holding its line pretty well. The varied cars in the race – Bristols, Rileys, a couple of Jowett Javelins, an Alvis 3-litre – were all pretty much in standard trim too and I won without much difficulty, setting fastest lap.

📷 *Guy Griffiths Collection*

⬆ For dashing around town I had a humble Standard 8, but I got Alf Francis to fit it with a well-tweaked Standard 10 engine. It was turned out in my green and cream colours, and was fitted with various extras like spotlights and wing mirrors. It also must have been the only Standard 8 in the world with Borrani wire wheels! Here it is creeping into shot while I am interviewed for TV outside The White Swan in Whitchurch.

📷 *Stirling Moss collection*

➔ My experiences with my Standard 8 led to the factory asking me to race a Standard 10 at the August 1955 Oulton Park meeting. Compared with the Mercedes-Benz W196 and 300SLR I was driving that season it felt pretty gutless, of course, but I managed to finish second in my class that day. Some way ahead was the class winner, my future Vanwall and Aston Martin team-mate Tony Brooks in, of all things, a three-cylinder two-stroke DKW.

📷 *LAT*

← This has to be the oldest car I have ever competed in, or should that be on? It's a 1903 single-cylinder Cadillac and I drove it on the 1952 London-to-Brighton veteran car run. The most astonishing thing about it was that the owner, Fred Bennett (seen at the wheel), bought it new. He had imported it himself from Michigan 49 years before and set himself up as the first Cadillac agent in Britain, and he kept it for the rest of his life. We had a good run to Brighton in dry weather, although before the start one of the bands in the two-speed epicyclic transmission was slipping and we had to adjust it.

📷 *Stirling Moss collection*

← I didn't actually race this car. But I had a lot of fun getting to grips with it in a demonstration on the dirt surface of the Cumberland oval at Parramatta Park when I was down-under for the 1956 Australian Tourist Trophy at Albert Park. It's the WM-Cooper-Holden, built and raced by Jack Myers, and it was a typical example of Australian make-do ingenuity. It consisted of an old Cooper Formula 2 chassis that had been wrecked by its previous owner, straightened out and fitted with a 2.4-litre Holden straight-six engine with a locally developed twin-cam cylinder head and six Amal carburettors. It certainly had more power than the Alta- and Bristol-powered F2 cars that I remembered. Jack built various successful one-off racing cars, ending up with a fearsome little device with two 650cc supercharged Triumph motorcycle engines. Sadly he was killed in it at Catalina Park in 1962.

📷 *Stirling Moss collection*

⬆ Always ready to try any form of motor sport at least once, I took part in the Kitching Trophy Trial on a bitterly cold Derbyshire day in February 1952. Trialling, where you have to get as far as possible up a hill in a muddy, slippery field, and where the cars rarely exceed walking pace, doesn't sound very difficult. But it's much harder than it looks, requiring judgement, co-ordination and delicate throttle control.

I borrowed a car built up by well-known ERA racer and all-round enthusiast Cuth Harrison. He called it a Harford – Harrison plus Ford – because, like most cars of its ilk, it used the sidevalve 1172cc Ford engine. It was extremely basic and light, and you sat right at the back to get as much weight as possible over the rear wheels. Just as your passenger in rallying is there to look after the navigation, so your passenger in trialling is there to bounce up and down when forward motion starts to diminish, to help the rear wheels to grip, so this was a different role for my friend John Cooper. We didn't do very well against the experts, but there were some more outsiders taking part, including racing driver Reg Parnell and journalist and commentator John Bolster, complete with his trade-mark deerstalker hat. We did manage to beat them.

📷 *LAT*

CHAPTER 6
STUTTGART ÜBER ALLES

By the end of 1953, after my disasters with the ERA and the Cooper-Altas – and indeed with BRM – I had realised that my goal of winning Formula 1 races in a British car was, as things were at the time, simply unattainable. It was an open secret that Mercedes-Benz were putting in place a return to Grand Prix racing, so Dad and my manager Ken Gregory flew to Stuttgart to plead with the awe-inspiring Mercedes competitions boss, Alfred Neubauer, to give me a test. Neubauer's reply was that he had noted my efforts in uncompetitive cars, but he couldn't gauge my true talent until I'd had the chance to show what I could do in something decent. So for 1954 we decided to run a privateer Maserati in F1, and how we got on with that is told in the next chapter.

My races in the 250F seemed to tell Neubauer what he wanted to know, because after Mercedes' half-season in 1954, when their W196 F1 car was in a class of its own, I was thrilled to be summoned by Neubauer in November with an offer to join the team for 1955. This was to be not only in F1 but also in World Sports Car Championship events with their new sports-racing car, the 300SLR. I was to race alongside Fangio, the reigning World Champion and acknowledged to be the best driver in the world, with seasoned veteran Karl Kling and newcomer Hans Herrmann also on the strength. When not needed by the team I was free to drive for anyone else, as I wished. I had a test at Hockenheim, and quickly realised that the professionalism and sheer substance of the Mercedes effort was unlike anything I had witnessed before. As I got out of the car, a polite Mercedes employee was waiting for me with a bowl of water and a towel. And – the water was hot. I signed.

During 1955 I benefited enormously from the guidance and experience of three very special men. Alfred Neubauer, an enormous figure physically and metaphorically, was pretty daunting at first, and a strict disciplinarian. But he was also a supremely intelligent team manager, and put everything together to give you the maximum chance of winning races. Away from the track he had a rumbustious sense of humour, and didn't mind a joke at his own expense. I discovered this when we were on a long, boring flight to Argentina for our first race. In mid-air Hans Herrmann and I suddenly heard our names being shouted urgently from the back of the plane: Neubauer had pretended to become stuck in the lavatory. He had, as one would expect, a secretary who was as strict and efficient as he was. He said to me once, with his rumbling laugh: 'My secretary, she is 42. I am going to exchange her for two secretaries aged 21.'

Another great influence was the team's technical chief, Rudi Uhlenhaut. Born of a German father and an English mother, he spoke perfect public-school English – but, more important, he was a top-class driver. His position at Mercedes meant he was too important to be allowed to race, but he was capable in test sessions of setting competitive times. So it was much easier to discuss with him details of a car's performance or handling, because he looked at things from a driver's point of view.

The greatest influence of all, of course, came from my team leader, Juan Manuel Fangio. I learned an inestimable amount from following in his wheel-tracks, and also from working with him as part of the team. He was a father figure to me, hugely experienced, a wonderful man to work with and, for a racing driver, extraordinarily unselfish. He didn't speak English and I didn't speak Spanish, but we managed to converse after a fashion in Italian. We never hid any knowledge from each other, as some team-mates do today: we were friends as well as team-mates, and my respect for him was total. I realise that comparisons across generations are impossible, but for me he is still the greatest racing driver of all time.

I learned an inestimable amount from following in Fangio's wheeltracks. He was a father figure to me.

The Mercedes-Benz W196 Grand Prix car had appeared in mid-1954 in two shapes, as a conventional open-wheeler and, for the faster tracks, with an all-enveloping body. But from the start of the 1955 season the streamliner was kept under wraps. The W196 was big and strong, and bristled with innovative ideas. Within the multi-tube space frame the straight-eight engine, with desmodromic valve gear and fuel injection, was canted to the right, almost onto its side, to give a low bonnet line and to allow the transmission to pass beside the driver to the rear-mounted five-speed gearbox. Huge finned drum brakes were mounted inboard front and rear. Brake dust, as well as the usual cocktail of oil and rubber, would coat the drivers' faces so that the white circles left by the goggles on our black grimy faces would give us 'panda eyes'.

In 1955 there were only six rounds of the Formula 1 World Championship, apart from Indianapolis, which was nominally on the list but didn't affect anything. Although Fangio won in Argentina, the intense heat gave me a fuel vaporising problem. Monaco saw a rare defeat when Fangio and I suffered engine failures. But thereafter we were able to score regular, almost monotonous, 1–2 finishes. Then came Aintree, and my first Grand Prix victory – in front of my home crowd, too. I had another unlucky retirement at Monza, but I ended the year a clear second in the World Championship.

In 1954 Mercedes had concentrated on Formula 1, but for 1955 they also introduced the 300SLR sports car, effectively a two-seater, 3-litre version of the W196. Its first race was the Mille Miglia, and after three months of personal preparation and with the utterly indispensable help of my passenger and navigator Denis Jenkinson, I scored the most important victory of my career.

At Le Mans I am convinced we would have won our battle with the Jaguar D-types quite easily. But in a horrifying and tragic accident one of our team cars, driven by the Frenchman Pierre Levegh, crashed into the crowd. It was a kind of racing traffic accident: Mike Hawthorn, having just lapped Lance Macklin's Healey, made a late decision to dive into the pits. Macklin had to swerve to avoid him just as Levegh was coming up behind at probably 150mph, and the Mercedes ran up the tail of the Healey, flew into the air and crashed into the crowd. His 300SLR burst into flames and broke in two, with the front half scything through the massed spectators, and 83 people, including Levegh, were killed. During the night, when Fangio and I had a four-lap lead, the order came from Stuttgart to withdraw. I've always regretted that, because Levegh's crash was through no fault of his own nor of Mercedes, and our withdrawal would not have brought back the dead. Mike, who had unwittingly initiated the chain reaction, won the race.

The 300SLR was only raced six times, and but for that withdrawal would have won six times. Of the remaining five, two were comparatively minor races in Sweden and at the Nürburgring, both of which Fangio won because Neubauer told me to stay behind. It wasn't an order, it was a request, and I complied. My three victories were the Mille Miglia, the Tourist Trophy and the Targa Florio, all proper road-race classics. Usually, I could never quite beat Fangio's times in the W196, but in the 300SLR I always felt I was that little bit quicker than him. I asked him about this once, and he just smiled and said, 'I always prefer to be able to see my front wheels.'

At the end of 1955, having won the World Championship and the World Sports Car Championship, Mercedes-Benz withdrew from racing, and I was back in Maseratis. I had only done a total of 13 races for the Untertürkheim team, six Grands Prix, one *formule libre* and six sports car races. But I had done more to establish myself in those 13 races than I could have believed possible when I'd signed 10 months before.

↑ A turning point in my career. Here I am at Hockenheim on 4 December 1954 in a Mercedes-Benz W196 Formula 1 car for the first time. Technical chief Rudolf Uhlenhaut is telling me how I can expect the car to behave, while the initially scary Mercedes racing boss Alfred Neubauer is already reading the riot act. Behind with his overcoat over his shoulders is Mercedes PR chief Artur Keser.

📷 *Getty Images*

↗ Getting a push start for that momentous test run, with Neubauer smiling benignly now. On this occasion the W196 was wearing a strange grille that was never used in racing. The road was damp and I didn't find the car immediately friendly to drive: it felt big and heavy, and you sat in the cockpit with your legs wide apart each side of the clutch housing behind the canted engine, with the throttle and brake pedals one side and the clutch pedal the other. But I got down to the same time that established team-mate Karl Kling had set in the dry, and Neubauer seemed pleased with that.

📷 *Getty Images*

→ After the test Neubauer offered me more money than I had ever been paid in my life: a healthy retainer, plus 90 per cent of all prize and bonus money earned, with 10 per cent going to the mechanics. After I signed, Dad and Neubauer and I drank a toast to the coming season. I was 25 years old, and I was being taken on by the world's top racing team, to drive alongside Fangio, the reigning World Champion. I knew I would learn a lot from him and from Mercedes.

📷 *Getty Images*

↑ First Grand Prix of the 1955 season was in Argentina, and in Buenos Aires January is high summer. The weather was simply stifling. Out on the track it was 55 degrees C, and in the cockpit of a racing car for three hours it was even hotter. Almost every driver suffered from debilitating heat exhaustion, and had to stop and hand over to a team-mate who'd come in for a breather. The one who didn't was Fangio, who told me afterwards that he kept going by imagining cool fountains plashing into a serene lake. I'm not sure how he could occupy his mind with that and still reel off 96 laps, including setting fastest lap – but then he was Fangio. Like everyone else I was suffering from the heat, but I managed to carry on and was lying second to Fangio when I got a vapour lock in the fuel system. Furious, I stopped out on the circuit – and the medics rushed up and tried to bundle me into an ambulance, assuming I was about to pass out. I fought them off and walked back to the pits, whereupon Neubauer sent me out in Hans Herrmann's car. I managed to bring it home fourth.

📷 *LAT*

→ Showing their determination to be winners whatever the cost, Mercedes made two special short-wheelbase cars for the tight twists of Monaco, with outboard front brakes. On the grid Fangio and I sandwiched the side-tank Lancia of Alberto Ascari. Eugenio Castellotti's Lancia, No 30, came through from row 2 and got ahead of me, but by lap 5 Fangio and I were running together in a comfortable 1–2.

📷 *Klemantaski Collection*

⬆ This was everyone's first sight of what came that year to be called 'The Train': Fangio and me dominating from the front in first and second places. It was to be the pattern throughout the season, but the Monte Carlo streets exposed a weakness that had not emerged during all of Mercedes' testing. A tiny screw in the valvegear broke on Fangio's car and punched a hole in the camshaft cover. All the oil leaked away, and his engine blew up.

📷 *LAT*

⬇ But I continued in the lead at Monaco, and with 20 minutes left to run I had almost lapped the entire field. Then to my dismay the same thing happened to me, and this shot shows me being followed up the hill to Casino Square by a plume of oily smoke. I stopped by the finish line and when the flag fell I pushed my car home ninth and last. Ascari took over the lead, only to have a mammoth accident when his Lancia got out of shape coming out of the tunnel, mounted the barriers and was catapulted into the sea. To everyone's relief, as the car sank like a stone, Ascari's blue helmet broke the surface and he swam strongly to the harbour wall. The double World Champion was completely unhurt – but four days later, testing a friend's car at Monza with a borrowed helmet, he crashed and was killed.
📷 *LAT*

← The old 8.7-mile Spa-Francorchamps road circuit, climbing and plunging through the Ardennes forests, was a wonderful place to let a Formula 1 car have its head, with a superb selection of long, fast corners like this one. Despite the tight hairpin before the start, we were averaging over 120mph. After Argentina and Monaco, this was the first race when our 1–2 held to the end, leaving the Ferraris a long way behind in our wake. If we were comfortably ahead at two-thirds distance Neubauer would hang out a pit signal saying 'REG'. That meant *regulare* – hold station – because he didn't want us racing at ten-tenths all the way if it wasn't necessary.

📷 *LAT*

↑ In the gravelly Zandvoort paddock as the teams arrive before the Dutch Grand Prix, my car (10) and Karl Kling's (12) are unloaded from one of the double-deck vans that brought them from the racing headquarters at Untertürkheim. Although Mercedes-Benz were the top Formula 1 team of their day, with the biggest budget, this photo shows how primitive everything was compared to today's serried ranks of huge transporters and motorhomes. The largest van in the paddock seems to be that of the Mintex brake linings people on the left.

📷 *Getty Images*

➔ In the Dutch Grand Prix 'The Train' ran to schedule once again, and after nearly three hours' racing Fangio and I finished 1–2, just 0.3sec apart. This photo shows how much oil and brake dust would accumulate during a long race on my aero screen, and on my face and overalls – not just from my car but also from Fangio's running a few yards in front.

📷 *LAT*

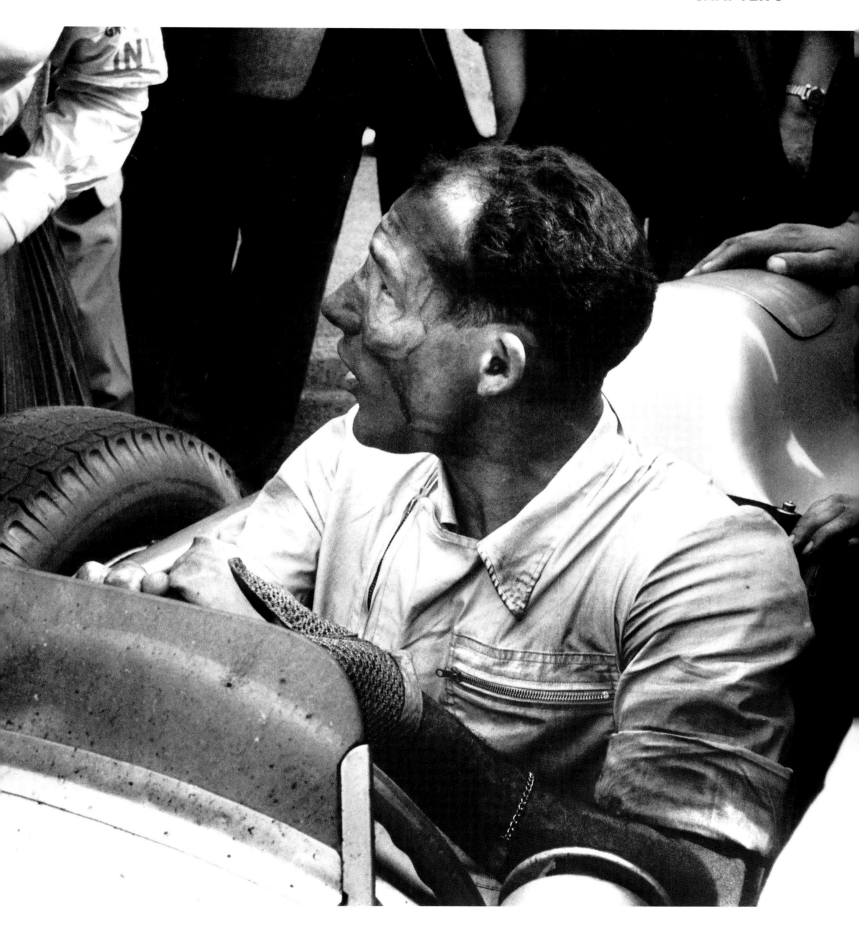

← Because of the Le Mans disaster the French Grand Prix was cancelled, so the next round was my own British Grand Prix, held that year at Aintree. By now Fangio and I had a really good working relationship: here we are comparing notes before the start.

📷 *Stirling Moss collection*

← Under the W196's bonnet a maze of pipework and wiring hid the straight-eight engine, which lay almost on its side, but the eight fuel injector pipes feeding into the top of the engine could clearly be seen.

📷 *LAT*

⬆ The British Grand Prix field gets away, with the Grand National horse-racing course and its very grand grandstands in the background. I qualified on pole, 0.2sec ahead of Fangio, and we leave the line side by side ahead of Jean Behra's gallant Maserati, which qualified third ahead of the other two W196s of Piero Taruffi and Karl Kling. Behind them are Harry Schell's Vanwall and Roberto Mières' Maserati.

📷 *LAT*

← Fangio and I had a great battle for the lead, passing and repassing, but then suddenly he was gone from my mirrors and was 11 seconds behind me. I had no idea why until nearly 60 years later, when a photographer who'd been shooting around the back of the circuit told me what had happened. Fangio made a most untypical mistake, sliding wildly across the grass, but managing to gather it all together without actually spinning. The photographer had seen it – although, would you believe, he was changing his film at the time and couldn't record it – but there were no other photographers or spectators at that point. Nowadays, when television cameras cover every inch of every corner, we'd know all about it.

📷 *Klemantaski Collection*

← As the race went into its final stages Mercedes were 1–2–3–4 with everyone else at least a lap down, so Neubauer, as expected, hung out the 'REG' sign. I eased my pace and Fangio closed up on me, but being a gentleman he obeyed the signal. Nevertheless, as we came out of the final corner with the chequered flag waiting, my right foot was absolutely flat to the floor, just in case. The timekeepers gave the official gap between us as a fifth of a second, but I think that's because in those days a fifth was the smallest measure their watches went down to. I didn't care what the gap was: I had scored my first Grand Prix victory, and I'd done it in my home race. It was a great day for me.
📷 *LAT*

⬇ After our victory Fangio was the first to congratulate me. I was never quite sure whether I'd beaten him fair and square that day, or whether he'd let me win because it was my home race. When I asked him, then and years later, he always just smiled enigmatically. But then he never told me about that moment across the grass…

There was only one race left in the World Championship season, at Monza, and if you do the maths you'll see that Fangio's second place at Aintree clinched his third World Championship title. But nobody noticed! All the headlines were about my win, because in those days people were more interested in race victories than boring championship points. It's very different today.
📷 *Daimler Archives*

↑ The streamliner bodies for the W196, which were used three times in 1954, weren't used again until the final race of 1955, the Italian Grand Prix at Monza with its dramatic new high-speed banked section. Mercedes took one of the previous year's long-wheelbase streamliners, and two medium-wheelbase streamliners made specially for this race. In practice we discovered that the new ones didn't cope so well with the banking, so the longer car was prepared for Fangio and, after a phone call to Untertürkheim, a new long-wheelbase streamliner was prepared for me and rushed down from Germany to Italy on the back of Mercedes' special high-speed transporter. It's seen here with an open-wheeler on the back, but it could also accommodate a streamliner or a 300SLR. Typical Mercedes: nothing was too much trouble if it would help you to win. It arrived in time for Saturday practice.

📷 *Daimler Archives*

→ The W196 streamliners make a wonderful sight thundering around the Monza banking, Fangio running just ahead of me as usual. But just before half-distance one of Fangio's back wheels flung up a substantial stone which shattered my aeroscreen. It was impossible to drive the car with the 180mph buffeting that ensued, so I rushed into the pits. Mercedes, of course, with their typical efficiency, had a spare screen ready in the pit in case one might be needed. If I'd been driving for Maserati there would have been an Italian opera while they scurried around looking for a new screen, and the race would have been over before they'd found it. My new screen was fitted very rapidly and I was on my way again, in eighth place. In my efforts to catch up I set a new Monza lap record, but just as I was moving into sixth place there was another rare Mercedes failure: the engine blew up due to a broken piston. That was my last Grand Prix for Mercedes-Benz – but I was second in the World Championship to Fangio, and I had enjoyed an utterly memorable season.

📷 *Getty Images*

← Denis Jenkinson and I prepared for the Mille Miglia relentlessly, first in my own Mercedes 220SE saloon, then at higher speed around the entire route in a 300SL Gullwing, and in sections in a 300SLR practice car. Gradually we built up a record of the entire 1000-mile route, which Jenks transposed onto an 18ft-long ribbon of paper that rolled behind the Perspex window of the sealed box we'd come up with. As voice communication was impossible in the sound and fury of the cockpit, we devised a simple language of 15 different hand signals so that he could indicate to me every corner, every serious bump, every hazard. Each corner was graded into one of three categories – Saucy, Dodgy and Very Dangerous – with a different hand signal for each type. The 300SLR carried two different-sized spare wheels (one for the front, one for the back) and we endlessly practised changing wheels, but as it turned out we didn't need them in the race. At one stage during our recce I spun the 300SLR practice car gently into a ditch after I hit a sheep wandering in the road. More serious was the damage done to this 300SL, when an Italian army truck turned across our bows. Mercedes gave us another Gullwing, took the wreck back to the factory and no doubt broke it up.

📷 *LAT*

← Before our race car was taken to Brescia for the start of the Mille Miglia, Jenks and I drove it on the road 100 miles or so from the factory to Hockenheim, and here we are about to do some fast laps to give it a thorough test. Jenks had been a sidecar rider with world champion motorcyclist Eric Oliver, so he was uniquely qualified to travel with me in a race. The seats had been tailor-made to fit us and Jenks had his own horn button, which not only blasted the air horns but also flashed the lights. Any other detail changes either of us wanted in the cockpit to help us in our long Italian day were immediately carried out. The W196s and 300SLRs all had quick-release four-spoke steering wheels, but I preferred three spokes. I always used the same three-spoke wheel while I was at Mercedes, and during pre-race preparation it would be transferred from car to car. Six decades later I still have it, hanging on my study wall.

📷 *Stirling Moss collection*

⬆ This picture gives some idea of the nature of the Mille Miglia route, all on public roads, with people coming out of their houses to watch unprotected by the side of the road, although some token straw bales were scattered about here and there. The crowds were as thick as this almost all the way around the entire 1000-mile route, thinning out a bit only up in the mountains. The roads were meant to be closed, but they couldn't be totally monitored the whole way, and there was always the chance that you'd come across a Fiat-load of enthusiasts going from one vantage point to another.
📷 *LAT*

← This shot of the 300SLR was taken early in the race, because it's still looking quite clean, although there is some straw in the air intake from a little brush with the bales in Padua. Later on we picked up some body damage to the right front near Pescara when, trying to pass a slow Gordini, I had a moment and had to mount a pavement and scraped a wall. While climbing the Radicofani Pass, a grabbing brake spun us into a ditch, denting the tail, but fortunately we were able to drive straight out again.

🖾 *Daimler Archives*

← Ten hours, seven minutes and 48 seconds after leaving Brescia at 7.22am, we storm into Brescia once more, having averaged nearly 98mph up and down mountains, through narrow village streets, and on fast stretches up to 170mph. And that included refuelling, fresh tyres at Rome, and slithering to a halt at each control to get our card stamped. On the 83-mile stretch from Cremona to Brescia, where the roads are fast and open, we'd averaged over 165mph. Fangio finished second, and we had beaten him by more than half an hour. It was without doubt the race of my life.

🖾 *Stirling Moss collection*

⬆ It's all over, I'm clutching a bunch of flowers, Jenks seems to have been given a couple of bottles of Haig's whisky, and we are both in need of a good bath. Before the race Fangio gave each of us one of his mysterious little pills. He didn't tell us what they were, but he said they would keep us going. Jenks decided not to take his, but I took mine. It certainly worked – after that bath and a meal I jumped into my Mercedes 220SE saloon and drove non-stop 400 miles to Stuttgart, getting there before dawn on Monday. I had a meeting with the Mercedes directors that morning and then drove back to England. Jenks kept his pill and had it analysed in England, but apparently it contained a strange South American ingredient that the chemists couldn't identify…

📷 *Getty Images*

← The 1955 Le Mans 24 Hours produced the worst motor racing disaster in history, and sadly the 300SLRs were pulled out of the race during the night on the factory's orders. I was paired with Fangio, but for some reason Neubauer decided he should start – I never found out why, because I was always quicker in a Le Mans start – so I was denied this great battle in the opening stages with Mike Hawthorn's D-type. This is Fangio slipstreaming Hawthorn on the Mulsanne Straight early in the race. Mike seems to be finding time to make his favourite V-sign to the photographer.
📷 *LAT*

↑ At Le Mans I wore different goggles, which I decided would be better than a visor if it rained. Here I am bringing our car into the pits at 2am, having been summoned in because word had come from the factory that the remaining 300SLRs should be withdrawn. The dent on the nose probably came from debris during the accident, for Fangio had to charge through smoke and flying wreckage as it was still happening. At this point we were leading the Hawthorn/Bueb Jaguar by almost four laps. Our 300SLR was running like clockwork, and there's no doubt in my mind that we would have won.

📷 *Stirling Moss collection*

← To combat the Jaguars' disc brakes during the long, hard race, Mercedes developed an ingenious air brake, seen here in action at the Esses. This involved the entire bodywork behind the driver, complete with headrest, hinging up hydraulically into the airstream when the driver pushed a fingertip lever. It worked extremely well, and we found we were able to out-brake the Jaguars at the end of the Mulsanne Straight. At the fast White House corner you just flicked up the air brake for a moment and didn't need to touch the brake pedal. In practice Jaguar's Lofty England complained to the organisers that when the air brake was in use we had no rearward vision, so Mercedes inserted a couple of Perspex panels that lined up with the mirror.

📷 *LAT*

⬆ Dundrod had been good to me, with two TT wins so far, and it was good to me again when the Mercedes team went there with three 300SLRs. The race lasted more than seven hours, and co-drivers were mandatory, so it was decided to pair me with John Fitch, who would do just enough laps in the middle of the race to satisfy the regulations. I had built up a big lead over Fangio when my right rear tyre burst dramatically, tearing away some of the bodywork. I got the car back to the pits and the mechanics hastily cut away some more of the damaged panel to make sure it cleared the wheel. Fitch rejoined in second place and then he dropped to third, but after 35 minutes I was back in the car again, and I stayed in it until the end. I was able to lead home a Mercedes 1–2–3, at least a lap ahead of everybody else, including the second-placed Fangio/Kling car.
📷 *LAT*

⬇ During Saturday practice for the Tourist Trophy it was cold and intermittently wet, and here I am trying to insulate Denis Jenkinson from the weather. Jenks was there to do his usual job of reporting on the race for *Motor Sport* magazine. After what we'd gone through together on the Mille Miglia, he and I had become staunch friends.
📷 *LAT*

↑ A fine view of the fast, narrow Dundrod road circuit. Behind me the third-placed 300SLR, driven by Wolfgang von Trips and André Simon, squeezes past a slow Triumph TR2, showing clearly the restricted road width and the varying speeds of the 49-car field. Three drivers were killed that year, and Dundrod was not used for car racing again.

📷 *Stirling Moss collection*

➜ The 1955 TT took place on my 26th birthday, so as I climbed out of the Mercedes after the finish somebody presented me with a cake. Mike Hawthorn came over for a slice, wearing his green anorak and his bow tie as always. He and local boy Desmond Titterington drove the lone works Jaguar D-type superbly, and it was cruel luck that they lost second place when the engine blew with only four laps to go.

📷 *LAT*

⬆ My last race for Mercedes-Benz was the wonderful Targa Florio in October, run over 13 laps of a 47-mile circuit of Sicilian public roads, some of them pretty primitive. Having won the Formula 1 World Championship with Fangio, Mercedes needed to win this race to wrest the World Sports Car Championship from Ferrari, and took it very seriously, bringing 56 people to Sicily. Here are four of the team gathered around a hack 220 saloon: my co-driver on this occasion, Peter Collins, and I have our arms round Hans Herrmann, and John Fitch is on the left. To learn the circuit thoroughly I spent a full day earlier in the week in a Gullwing 300SL doing 12 high-speed laps, a distance of 560-odd miles. Quite hairy, because of course the roads were open.
📷 *LAT*

➜ The Targa circuit is wonderfully exciting, and often treacherous. I had been suffering from a nasty dose of flu and had barely slept the night before the race, but from the start I built up a good lead over Castellotti's Ferrari. Then a sudden rainstorm up in the hills coated the road with mud and I slid off, walloped a wall, then went down a bank into a field. Several Sicilian locals rushed to my aid, and with much heaving from them and revving from me we eventually got the 300SLR back on the road.
📷 *Stirling Moss collection*

↑ My off-road escapade lost us 12 minutes, and I didn't know how much damage I'd done, so I came straight into the pits. In this shot I am leaping out to hand over to Peter Collins, and the mechanics are checking quickly for any serious damage at the offside front. Peter did a great job getting the car back into the lead, although he hit a wall and crunched the left front wing, matching my damage to the other front corner.

📷 *Daimler Archives*

↗ This is me on my final stint. The poor old SLR looks pretty battered, but the car's strength was proved once again because it was going as well as ever, and I was able to get under the lap record to seal our win over the Fangio/Kling 300SLR. It was a hectic but ultimately very satisfying end to my Mercedes-Benz season.

📷 *Daimler Archives*

→ The team lines up for an end-of-term team photograph after the Targa: from left, John Fitch, Desmond Titterington, Peter Collins and me, then Alfred Neubauer, whom we all now regarded as a benevolent uncle, then Fangio and Karl Kling.

📷 *Stirling Moss collection*

⬆ That wasn't quite the end of my Mercedes driving career, because I twice did the Tour de France in 300SL Gullwings. The Tour was a serious event, lasting six days and taking in circuits, hillclimbs and rally stages all over France, with road sections in between. In 1956 I did it in a works-prepared car, with French rally man Georges Houel as my passenger. We were dogged by a misfire, but we still finished second to Fon de Portago's Ferrari. In 1957 I did it in my own 300SL road car, seen here. My navigator this time was *The Autocar* sports editor Peter Garnier, who'd taken over that job after poor John Cooper had been killed in a road accident. Although the Ferraris were much quicker now, Peter and I survived a water leak to finish fourth.
📷 *LAT*

⬇ A final Mercedes story: here I am with the American actress Claudia Hall, whom I got to know during 1955. An unfortunate incident with her got us into the papers. She was flying into Heathrow on a late-night flight, and I went to pick her up in a factory 300SL Gullwing that Rudi Uhlenhaut had lent me. It was quite special, because it was a development car with a low-pivot swing rear axle as on the racers, a feature that later appeared on the production 300SLs when the Roadster came out. At about 1am, as I was bringing Claudia back from the airport, a lunatic came over a red light smack into us. We were both fortunately unhurt, but the 300SL was a write-off. I called Stuttgart, and they rushed over and took the car away. I heard nothing more about it.

📷 *Stirling Moss collection*

CHAPTER 7
MY ITALIAN JOB

As recounted earlier, by the start of the 1954 season I had despaired of finding a British single-seater capable of winning Grands Prix. With Neubauer's words about needing to prove myself in a decent car ringing in our ears – and with no vacant seats to go for in the Ferrari and Maserati teams, which were dominating Formula 1 in those pre-Mercedes days – Dad, my manager Ken Gregory and I decided the right thing to do was to buy a competitive car and run it privately. Maserati agreed to sell us one of their 250F single-seaters, for the dizzy sum of £5500. Some of this would come from Shell-Mex & BP, which was my fuel and oil sponsor, and Dad guaranteed the rest, on the strict understanding that it would have to be paid back out of my future earnings.

Alf Francis was despatched to Modena in March to oversee the car's construction, and he infuriated the Maserati people by insisting on various changes that I required. These included altering the tubes over the driver's knees to get the steering wheel further forward for my straight-arm driving position, and moving the central throttle pedal to the right.

As soon as I got my hands on my 250F I realised it was in a different class compared with the Coopers and Connaughts I'd been used to. Its twin-cam six gave a torquey 240bhp, and its handling was a joy, predictable and progressive. Ours was very much a private entry, looked after by Alf and Tony Robinson, who took it to events in our little Commer van. In its pale green livery it looked very different from the gleaming red works line-up, led by Fangio and his countryman and protégé, Onofre Marimón. We decided that, while the works cars ran to a rev limit of 8000rpm, I would stick to 7200rpm: this would put me at a disadvantage, but we hoped it would bring greater reliability and fewer expensive engine rebuilds.

During that spring and early summer I raced my Maser on my own account seven times, including the Belgian and

British Grands Prix. In the Belgian race I finished third, earning my first World Championship points, and by now the Maserati team manager, Nello Ugolini, was watching my efforts closely. In August, during first practice for the German Grand Prix, I lapped 8sec under Ascari's lap record, and that obviously made a further impression. That afternoon Ugolini sat me down and proposed that my car should henceforth be run as a works entry. Great! This was what I'd been waiting for. Overnight my car was hastily brush-painted red, but leaving a green band around the nose – and now I could use 8000rpm, because any engine rebuilds would be down to the factory. That made a huge difference. Fangio had moved across to Mercedes in July, and sadly poor Onofre Marimón was killed during that German GP weekend, so suddenly I found myself regarded as effectively the Maserati team leader.

I won some British Formula 1 races during the rest of that season but I had no joy in the remaining Grands Prix, although victory, against the might of Mercedes, came heart-stoppingly close at Monza. For 1955 I was with Mercedes, of course, but my contract with them allowed me to race other cars when their schedule permitted. So I kept my 250F, and raced it when I could in British events. As we wanted the car to earn its keep when I wasn't around, we entered it for other drivers – Lance Macklin, John Fitch, Bob Gerard and notably Mike Hawthorn. In January 1956 we also took it down-under for the New Zealand Grand Prix, which I won.

After Mercedes' departure I was in quite a strong position to put myself on the Formula 1 market for the 1956 season. Still hoping for a British car that would be strong enough to be a consistent winner, I tested for Connaught, BRM – who had a new, much simpler four-cylinder 2½-litre car – and Vanwall. It was Vanwall who looked the most promising, and I actually did a race for them in May.

As soon as I got my hands on my 250F I realised it was in a different class compared with what I had been used to.

But in the end I took Maserati's offer to be confirmed as their team leader, not only in Formula 1 but also in sports car racing, for which they had a strong car in the 300S. In Formula 1 my fees were £500 per Grand Prix, £300 per non-championship race, and 60 per cent of prize and bonus money. In sports car races I got 60 per cent of the start money and all of the prize money and bonuses. Plus I was free to drive for whom I chose in any races Maserati didn't enter – always something I stuck out for when negotiating any contract – and that would give me the chance to do several major sports car races for Aston Martin.

It turned out to be a hectic season, with plenty of ups and downs. But it brought me two World Championship Grand Prix victories. My Monaco win, leading from flag to flag, was particularly satisfying: it was a proper three-hour, 100-lap race in those days. The other win, at Monza, was far from being as straight-forward.

I've never set that much store by championship points (apart from in 1958, when I must admit I did get caught up in all that). To me it was always winning a race that mattered, not adding up points at the end of the season. But in 1956 I did end the year second in the World Championship to Fangio, as I had done the previous year and as I would do the following year.

In sports cars, Maserati's 300S was rather like a 3-litre, wide-bodied version of the 250F, and in its own way was every bit as good. I loved it, and it may be my favourite sports-racing car ever. In 1956 I did seven races in these beautifully balanced cars and won five, came second in one (when I took over another car after mine had broken) and had one retirement. It was a wonderfully effective piece of kit.

For the Mille Miglia, Maserati came up with a bigger car, the 350S, with a dry-sumped version of their 3½-litre production car engine, de Dion rear end and five-speed rear-mounted Colotti gearbox. With 290bhp it was quicker than the 300S, but much harder to drive. The chassis, being developed for the big V8-powered 450S on which Maserati were pinning their future hopes, was a lot heavier, and after the 300S it felt unwieldy. As you will see on the following pages, our Mille Miglia that year certainly did not repeat our previous year's success, and I didn't race it again.

That 450S was Maserati's 1957 attempt to build a really powerful sports-racer that would deal with Ferrari once and for all. Powerful it certainly was, with nearly 400bhp from its thunderous four-cam V8. It only survived one season because from 1958 the FIA, worried that sports-car engine sizes would just go on getting bigger, imposed a 3-litre limit. The 450S was incredibly quick when it was going: it was a genuine 185mph car, reaching 100mph from a standing start in little more than 10 seconds. But its sheer heft exposed various weaknesses. I did six races in the 450S and retired in all but one, with clutch, gearbox, half-shaft and other maladies. We did win the six-hour Swedish Sports Car Grand Prix, in which I drove both 450Ss entered. The most embarrassing outing was the Mille Miglia, when my brake pedal snapped off after only seven miles. If that wasn't bad enough, the coupé version that was hastily prepared for the Le Mans 24 Hours was possibly the most unpleasant car I ever raced. I for one didn't mourn the 450S's passing.

The big V8 was also used in a single-seater device called the Eldorado Special, paid for by an Italian ice-cream magnate to take on the visiting Indycar drivers on the Monza banking for the so-called Race of Two Worlds in 1958. This car did its level best to kill me, so that's another Maserati that I don't remember with affection. But the 250F and the 300S were superbly balanced, hugely enjoyable racing cars – just like the other Maserati that I liked very much, the so-called Birdcage, which came a few years later.

⬆ My first victory with my privateer Maserati 250F came in the Aintree 200 in May 1954. It was the first time the Liverpool track beside the Grand National horse-racing course had been used, running in an anti-clockwise direction. This was a *formule libre* race with a very mixed field, including Peter Collins in the 4½-litre Ferrari Thin Wall Special, Ron Flockhart in the Mk2 V16 BRM – a slightly less woeful machine than the Mk1 I'd briefly raced two years earlier – and Reg Parnell's Formula 1 Ferrari. I was third in my heat behind Parnell and Collins, and before the final I got Alf Francis to change the carburettor choke and jet sizes, which definitely improved the car's performance on that track. In the final, from the second row of the grid, I took the lead from Collins soon after half-distance. As he fell back I ran out the winner by 48 seconds from Parnell and Flockhart. Alf's pit board is showing me the top three places and tells me there are five laps to go.

📷 *LAT*

→ The 1954 Belgian Grand Prix at Spa was a very important race for me. The old Spa circuit consisted of 8.7 miles of very fast public roads through the Ardennes forests, the sort of track that I always loved. Sticking to my self-imposed rev limit I qualified ninth. Fangio's works 250F took pole and his team-mate Onofre Marimón qualified fourth, with the Ferraris of González and Farina between them. In the race others had problems but my privateer 250F went perfectly, and I came through to finish third behind Fangio and Maurice Trintignant's Ferrari. Here I am accelerating out of the La Source hairpin at the top of the hill before the old start line.

📷 *LAT*

→ Stirling Moss Ltd was the name of our little team, and here it is in its entirety before the start of the Belgian Grand Prix. On the left is our brilliant but often acid-tongued Polish chief mechanic Alphons Frantisek Kowaleski, known to one and all as Alf Francis, and on the right our young No 2 mechanic Tony Robinson, who spent his working life in motor racing and ended up running BRP, the British Racing Partnership – of which more later.

📷 *LAT*

← I was determined to put on a good show in front of my home crowd in the British Grand Prix at Silverstone, and I qualified on the outside of the front row. The flag has just fallen and González has made a blinder of a start in his Ferrari. The rest of us are, from left, Fangio (Mercedes streamliner), Jean Behra (Gordini), Karl Kling (Mercedes), Mike Hawthorn (Ferrari) and me. When things settled down it was González and Fangio at the front, and then Mike and me disputing third place. As the race went on I shook Mike off, and then I managed to get past Fangio and was in a secure second place with just 10 laps to go when a drive shaft broke. Sickening.

📷 *Stirling Moss collection*

← It rained hard mid-race and the track was almost flooded in places. This shows the featureless nature of the old ex-airfield Silverstone, with a few marker barrels marking out the corners. Fangio hit several barrels, denting both front corners of the streamliner. I have to own up: I caught one with my right front wheel, too.

📷 *Getty Images*

⬆ Here I am at Oulton Park in August, surrounded by a typically well-behaved British crowd. I'd entered my own 250F for this British non-championship Formula 1 race, the Gold Cup, but after the Belgian, British and German Grands Prix it was in dire need of an overhaul. The previous weekend at the Nürburgring Maserati had officially nominated me as a team member, so they took my car back to Modena and sent a factory car to Oulton for me. But it didn't make the trip up from Italy in time for practice, so I had to start at the back of the 19-car grid. I was seventh at the end of lap 1, second on lap 3 and was leading by lap 4. I won from Reg Parnell's Ferrari by almost a lap. I won the 20-lap *formule libre* race, too, and then jumped into the Beart Cooper and won an hour-long Formula 3 race. All in a day's work.

📷 *LAT*

↑ The 1954 Italian Grand Prix was very nearly a magical day. I was leading a great Italian team on Italian soil, and the three top teams in Formula 1 were represented on the front row – Fangio in the Mercedes, Ascari in the Ferrari adjusting his goggles before the off, and me in the Maserati doing the same. Kling's Mercedes is behind. After an hour and a half's racing Ascari was leading, Fangio was second, I was third. I was able to tow past Fangio and close up on Ascari, who then dropped out with a blown engine. So, after 50 of the 80 laps, I was leading the Italian Grand Prix, and there didn't seem to be anything Fangio could do about it.
📷 *Getty Images*

↗ With 20 laps to go I was 20 seconds in front. Then, with 12 laps left, I noticed my oil pressure was fluctuating, and I could see in my mirrors a haze behind me. I dived into the pits and took on three gallons of oil – most of which ran straight out again onto the pit lane. The oil tank had split. I rejoined the race, but soon my oil-starved engine seized. I coasted almost to within sight of the finish line, and then I got out and pushed my silent, broken 250F up to the finish line. When I got there I sat on the tail and waited for Fangio to win the race, and then shoved it over the line to be classified 10th. But my efforts had made their mark: after the race Fangio said in his typically generous-hearted way that the race should rightfully have been mine. And Pirelli, whose tyres I was using, paid me the same bonus that would have been due if I'd won.
📷 *LAT*

→ I led Fangio again in the final Grand Prix of the year, at Barcelona, although Mercedes were having a bit of an off day: when this picture was taken we were only disputing fourth place. I retired with a holed piston, while Fangio finished third, a lap behind. This was the second and last time the Pedralbes circuit, on public streets on the edge of the city, was used for a World Championship Grand Prix. Some four miles long, it incorporated a very long straight along the Avenida del Generalísimo Franco, just in case we forgot who was in charge.
📷 *LAT*

↑ I liked my own Maserati to keep earning, and when I was otherwise engaged I would lend it to drivers who I thought could make good use of it. I was unable to take part in the Crystal Palace Formula 1 race in August 1955 because Mercedes were conducting endurance tests with the 300SLR at the Nürburgring. So I nominated Mike Hawthorn to drive it, and I returned from Germany that morning just in time to watch the race. Here Mike and I are having a pre-race pow-wow while the long-suffering Alf, reckoning he's heard it all before, looks into the middle distance. In those days drivers who raced each other weekend in, weekend out, were friends, and Mike and I remained so even during our tense World Championship battle in 1958. Mike did a good job for me that day: he beat Harry Schell's Vanwall by 1.4 seconds to win.

📷 *Stirling Moss collection*

➜ The following month Mike and I were lining up in opposition on the grid for the Oulton Park Gold Cup. Here Mike's side-tank Lancia-Ferrari is on pole beside my works 250F, Luigi Musso's 250F and Eugenio Castellotti's Lancia. As the flag fell Castellotti led briefly, but I was leading halfway round lap 1 and was able to stay there to win my second Gold Cup, over a minute ahead of Mike.

📷 *LAT*

↑ The Easter Monday meeting at Goodwood was traditionally the first big British meeting of the season, and in 1956 the 80-mile Formula 1 race produced a great Maserati/Connaught/BRM scrap. Mike Hawthorn in the new BRM P25 led initially, then Archie Scott Brown in the Connaught got past him, followed by me. Archie was born with malformed legs and a short right arm with no hand, but his car control was always prodigious, and so was his will to win. Driving brilliantly, with me watching his every move from a few feet behind, he led until his brakes started to fade, and I was able to get past. He hung on, but a leaking cam cover starved his engine of oil, and as we dived down into Woodcote his crank broke and he spun onto the grass. Then Hawthorn's BRM turned over at Fordwater when a driveshaft UJ seized, fortunately without hurting him, so I was left with an easy win.

I could see Archie leaning against his car smoking a cigarette and watching the race, so on my slowing down lap I stopped and gave him a lift back to the paddock. The crowds in the grandstand gave him a big round of applause. Archie was a great racer and a remarkable character, and I was much saddened when he died at Spa two years later.
📷 *LAT*

→ The 1956 Monaco Grand Prix was a race where everything ran perfectly to plan. Fangio, now team leader at Ferrari with their Lancia-derived side-tank cars, beat me to pole by 0.6sec, so I was sandwiched between him and Castellotti's Ferrari, but I got to the Gasworks Hairpin first and I came out first. From then on my task was to race on for three hours round the Monte Carlo streets with Fangio, who took over Peter Collins' Ferrari after his own broke its clutch, keeping up the pressure all the way. My Maserati didn't miss a beat, and I completed my 100th and final lap with Fangio still 6.1 seconds behind. It was my second-ever victory in a World Championship Grand Prix, after Aintree in 1955, and it felt really good.
📷 *LAT*

↑ The 1956 Belgian Grand Prix at Spa was a disappointment. Fangio's V8 Ferrari was quicker than my 250F along Spa's long straights, even though my car had revised bodywork with a longer nose and higher cockpit sides. But I was holding a comfortable second place behind him when, rushing uphill out of Eau Rouge, my left rear hub broke. The wheel flew off into the trees and disappeared. I managed to get my Formula 1 tricycle stopped without hitting anything, left it by the side of the track, and sprinted back to the pits, where Ugolini called in Cesare Perdisa and I took over his car.

I rejoined in sixth place, and was able to get up to third by the end, behind the Ferraris of Collins and Paul Frère. Meanwhile Fangio had retired with a comprehensively blown engine, so this was a race I could so easily have won. In the picture I am rounding La Source in Perdisa's old-shape 250F, in which I managed to set a new outright lap record. Fastest lap mattered in those days, because you earned a championship point for it. If you had been delayed and were going to finish out of the points, that was an excellent incentive to keep you motoring hard.
📷 *LAT*

→ Although I had great affection for the 250F, and enjoyed some fine races with it, sometimes things just didn't work out. From my Spa experience I knew that it wasn't as fast as the Ferraris in a straight line, and the high-speed triangle at Reims, the French Grand Prix venue, was mostly straight-line stuff. Maserati responded to this by producing an all-enveloping car, but in practice I found it didn't work very well and opted to race the long-nose car I'd used at Spa. It wasn't really on the pace, and I was in a disappointing eighth place when the gearlever snapped off. Once again poor old Perdisa was summoned in and I took over his car, only to find that the cockpit was awash with oil. I plugged on and managed to salvage fifth place. The only concession on his old-shape 250F to the high-speed track was a lip over the air intake.
📷 *LAT*

→ I really needed a good result in the Italian Grand Prix at Monza. The British Grand Prix at Silverstone had been a disaster: I led from pole and set fastest lap, then the fuel tank split and the back axle broke. In the German Grand Prix I finished second, but I couldn't stay with Fangio's Ferrari around the Nürburgring. For their home race Maserati rose to the occasion with a new car. The engine was angled across the chassis so that the prop shaft passed down the left of the cockpit, which allowed me to sit eight inches lower, beside the transmission instead of on top of it. This reduced the frontal area and lowered the centre of gravity.

In the early stages the Ferraris of Luigi Musso and Eugenio Castellotti led until they shredded their tyres, and Harry Schell also had a spell at the front in the increasingly rapid Vanwall. Soon, as this photo shows, Fangio and I were disputing the lead, until Fangio stopped with a steering problem. That left me with a really good lead, and it started to look as though the race was going my way…

📷 *Getty Images*

⬇ But with five laps to go, to my dismay, my engine coughed and died. Somebody's calculations had been wrong and I was out of fuel! As my car coasted down to walking pace I looked desperately over my shoulder and saw coming up behind me Luigi Piotti's privateer 250F, which was circulating in a lonely sixth place three laps down. I gestured frantically to him, and he twigged at once. He fell into my wheel tracks and nudged the tail of my Maser with the nose of his, punting me along until I was able to coast into the pits. The boys sloshed in half a dozen precious gallons to get me to the end of the race, and I rejoined in second place behind Musso's Ferrari. His car promptly obliged by throwing a tread and breaking its steering. But Fangio was coming up fast behind me, having taken over Peter Collins' Ferrari. I held him off to win by six seconds. It had been a busy afternoon.

📷 *LAT*

↑ Driving a big sports racer in the stifling heat of an Argentine summer is tiring work. This is me after scoring Maserati's first World Sports Car Championship win in the Buenos Aires 1000Kms. Being congratulated by Fangio is my Argentinian co-driver Carlos 'Charlie' Menditéguy, who as well as being a pretty useful driver was also a top polo player, a professional standard tennis player and a scratch golfer. After six and a half hours' racing we beat all the Ferraris by two laps or more.

📷 *Getty Images*

↑ As a Maserati works driver, I was often lent one of their beautiful little 2-litre road cars to run around in. Jenks took this shot, probably when we were meeting up to do some Mille Miglia practising: his Porsche is parked alongside.

📷 *LAT*

← After my Mille Miglia win for Mercedes the previous year, I had plenty to live up to in 1956. So Maserati built me a special car, with a 3½-litre engine in the heavier chassis they were developing for the 450S. I took Jenks with me again, but the build of the new car, aggravatingly, was way behind schedule, so we did our practising – 2500 miles in two and a half days – in a 300S.

The 350S was only finished literally the day before the race, and all I could do was try it up the road. It was definitely faster than the 300S, but didn't handle nearly as well, and was much less forgiving. Come the race I was grappling with strong understeer, and I found that at anything over 150mph the car wandered around all over the road. But the crowds lining the route were as enthusiastic and warmly motivating as ever, and we pressed on as hard as we could.

📷 *TopFoto*

➜ Then it started to rain heavily. Soon the cockpit of our hastily finished car was full of water, and Jenks and I were sitting in a muddy bath. At the Pescara control somebody shouted that we were in sixth place, but up into the Abruzzi mountains the car was slithering all over the road. Diving down into a sharp right-hander the front wheels locked under braking and I lost control. Afterwards Jenks took this picture of the scene: we went at considerable speed up the bank on the right, then back across the road and straight through the fence into thin air.

📷 *LAT*

➜ The car dived down the mountainside, and it was very fortunate that we happened to hit the only tree in sight. That stopped us from continuing steeply down for several hundred feet to the river far below, and probably rolling over and over. Neither of us was hurt, but somewhere during the accident we'd gone through a barbed wire fence, which had dug into my goggles and helmet and even scratched the face of my watch. I wish we'd persuaded Maserati to let us do the race in a good old 300S.

📷 *Stirling Moss collection*

← I got back into the 300S with great relief for the Nürburgring 1000Kms, paired this time with the tough little Frenchman Jean Behra. This was a long race: around the tortuous Nürburgring it would last nearly eight hours. I took the lead from the start and Jean kept it, so everything was looking good. Then, three hours into the race, the rear suspension broke. Jean nursed the stricken car back to the pits, Ugolini brought in the No 2 car of Piero Taruffi/Harry Schell and Jean rejoined in that.

All this put the Fangio/Castellotti Ferrari into a pretty comfortable lead. With two hours to run I got back in the car, 66 seconds behind Fangio. This was the sort of challenge I loved, especially around a circuit as demanding as the 'Ring. Gradually I wound him in, and when he took his final refuelling stop I was through and away. The picture shows me taking the flag about 25 seconds clear of the Old Man's Ferrari.

📷 *LAT*

↓ Maserati didn't make ugly racing cars, or – remembering the 450S Le Mans coupé coming up on page 169 – not very often. The 250F in its early and later forms was the archetypal mid-1950s single-seater, and this is the 300S showing its elegant nose, faired headlights, driver's headrest and rounded tail as I win the sports car race supporting the 1956 British Grand Prix at Silverstone. Up against the works Aston Martins it was in a class of its own, and I took pole, won the race and set fastest lap. I lapped everyone except Roy Salvadori, who was second in his Aston Martin DB3S.

📷 *Stirling Moss collection*

↑ I always loved going to the Bahamas races in December, because they provided a relaxed footnote to a hard season. I liked the place so much that I built a house there. In the 1956 Nassau Trophy Bill Lloyd, with whom I'd won Sebring in 1954 in Briggs Cunningham's Osca, lent me his own Maserati 300S. It was quite tired – allegedly it had done 33,000 miles of racing and road fun – and then Bill shunted it against a spinning back-marker in a previous race that weekend. The front was hastily patched up with sticky tape and strips of tin cut from empty oil cans, and the old dog went well for me. I was sufficiently far ahead of Masten Gregory's second-placed Testa Rossa Ferrari to come in for a quick drink of water, and a quick drink of oil for the car, averaging 96.2mph for over two hours. The 300S remains one of my all-time favourite sports-racing cars.

📷 *Stirling Moss collection*

← At one of the Nassau parties I met a beautiful American actress called Louise King. She was tremendous fun. The following February she was starring in *The Seven Year Itch* at the Coconut Playhouse in Miami. When Peter Collins told me he was passing through Miami on his way to the Cuban race we were all doing, I told him he should look her up.

Pete introduced himself to Louise on the Monday and took her out to dinner, asked her to marry him on the Wednesday, and they were married on the following Monday just before she had to go on stage for the evening performance. Pete always was a fast worker. He and Louise were a golden couple and they fitted together wonderfully. They were very happy until his dreadful fatal accident in the German Grand Prix 18 months later.

📷 *Stirling Moss collection*

⬆ At the 1956 German Grand Prix there was a 100-mile supporting race for sports cars under 1500cc, and Maserati came up with a lovely little four-cylinder 150S for me. I qualified on pole but made a bad start, and initially my Maser had a misfire that then cleared itself. Here I have finally just got past Roy Salvadori's 'bob-tail' Cooper-Climax, which proved to have much better brakes. I then closed to within 3 seconds of Hans Herrmann's winning Porsche. It was a fun way to spend an hour and a quarter before the serious 3 hours 40 minutes of the Grand Prix that afternoon.

📷 *LAT*

← In February 1957 a 300-mile sports-car race was organised in Cuba, on a street circuit on the outskirts of Havana. Maserati decided to send a 450S for Fangio and me to share, but it was held up by a dock strike in New York. So I was put in a borrowed 200S owned by the Venezuelan-domiciled Italian Ettore Chimeri, and the picture shows me hustling this little car though the bumpy streets, watched by the completely unprotected crowd.

After five laps the engine seized, so I trotted back to the makeshift pits and took over Harry Schell's 300S, which Harry had borrowed from a Brazilian. That dropped a valve. Fangio won, in somebody else's Maserati 300S. Cuba under President Batista was certainly different: we were all assigned armed bodyguards carrying .45 revolvers. The night before the race some of us thought it might be fun to go to a boxing match, and when the local hero was beaten there was a riot, with shots fired.

📷 *LAT*

↓ With their big V8 450S, Maserati attempted to replicate the success of the 300S and at the same time keep up in the power race against Ferrari. It was a real monster, and I never liked it. It was certainly quick, but it rarely held together over a long race. This was my first outing, the 1957 Buenos Aires 1000Kms, when Fangio and I shared a lone 450S entry. The race was held on the very bumpy and foolishly dangerous Costanera circuit: the long straight was up one side of a dual carriageway and down the other, giving closing speeds of around 320mph.

The thundering, grumbling 450S was so much faster than everything else that after 10 laps I had a minute's lead over Masten Gregory's Ferrari, and continued to pull away at that rate until I handed over to Fangio, who carried on the good work. We had the race in the bag when the clutch went, and though Juan continued without it, eventually the gearbox broke. Later on I took over the fourth-placed Behra/Menditéguy 300S, and worked hard to get it up to second place and prevent a Ferrari 1–2.

📷 *Stirling Moss collection*

↑ Of course Maserati wanted me to tackle the Mille Miglia in the big 450S, and they'd prepared it carefully, even fitting an additional two-speed gearbox in front of the main 'box at the back, to give me a choice of ratios to suit the mountains and the flat-out plains. Jenks came with me as usual, and having found out during our practice forays that the car really was phenomenally fast, we had high hopes of another victory. My picture shows us turning up for the start in the clean and gleaming car; note the big ducts to cool the front brakes. We seemed to be race favourites, and I was raring to go. But this was to be the 450S's worst humiliation.

We had travelled just seven of our 1000 miles when, approaching a sharpish left-hander at about 145mph, I hit the brakes and we slowed initially, and then seemed to accelerate again as my foot went straight to the floor. Incredibly the pedal, as I pushed it, had snapped off at its base. Somehow I slowed the car by changing down several gears and we scrabbled around the corner, and when I'd got it down to walking pace Jenks and I leapt out and stopped it by hand.

I wouldn't get another chance to score a second Mille Miglia win. About 40 miles from the finish Fon de Portago's Ferrari burst a tyre at 150mph and crashed into the crowd. Fon, his passenger Ed Nelson and nine spectators were killed. The race was never run again.

📷 *TopFoto*

⬆ Maserati came up with another secret weapon for the Le Mans 24 Hours. Looking for ultimate speed down the Mulsanne Straight, they got the British aerodynamicist Frank Costin to design a coupé body for the 450S. Whether or not it would have worked had it been built to Frank's specification we will never know, but in a typical Italian panic the car was thrown together at the last minute and was nothing like race-ready. The full-length undertray, a crucial part of Frank's thinking, was never fitted. The car arrived at the circuit with no windscreen wipers, and the ones that were hastily rigged up simply lifted off the screen at any speed. The throttle was sticking, and the lights – so important in a 24-hour race – barely seemed to penetrate their Perspex covers. Worst of all, there was no cockpit ventilation at all.

In the opening stages of the race I got up to second behind Hawthorn's Ferrari, but the car had a bad vibration, and was filling the cockpit with oily smoke, almost asphyxiating me. After managing to stay in the top three for two very uncomfortable hours I handed over to Harry Schell, who was in again a few laps later with a broken oil pipe. Once that had been mended a rear universal joint gave way and that, to my considerable relief, was that. The 450S coupé was never raced again, although I heard later that an eccentric American millionaire bought it and had it converted to a road car. Good luck to him.

📷 *Klemantaski Collection*

↑ This lady was a model called Valerie Agnew, and we're having dinner at a favourite watering hole of mine, the Colony Restaurant in Berkeley Square. Leslie 'Hutch' Hutchinson, a very successful entertainer of the day and a great favourite of Princess Margaret, used to sing at a white grand piano, but I just liked it as a nice place to spend an evening.

Stirling Moss collection

← This was another big, hairy Maserati and I always remember it as the car that tried very hard to kill me. In 1958 the Race of Two Worlds pitted the American Indianapolis roadsters against a handful of Europeans on the Monza banked bowl, running anti-clockwise. The Eldorado Special was a single-seater Maserati paid for by Gino Zanetti, boss of the Eldorado ice-cream manufacturer, and carrying his company logo in an early example of overt sponsorship. In a modified 250F chassis it used a 4.2-litre version of the big V8, running on alcohol. The car was very fast, but distinctly lively over the bumps on the banking. The race was run over 500 miles, divided into three heats, and once I had settled down into this very different style of racing I was able to run with some of the quickest of the Indy drivers, who of course were much more used to this sort of thing. In the first two heats I was fourth and then fifth, having a very hairy ride all the way.

In the third heat I was chasing A.J. Foyt high on the banking, doing about 175mph, when suddenly the steering wheel spun lifeless in my hands and I had no control at all. The Eldorado charged the retaining barrier at the top of the banking, bending it right back but fortunately not clearing it, and then spun along it, knocking down three concrete posts, tearing off a wheel and bursting two tyres. The accident went on and on, but finally the wrecked car spun back down the banking and came to a halt at the bottom in a huge cloud of dust. I got out of the remains and walked back to the pits. It had been a most unpleasant moment, and I realised I'd had a very lucky escape. But in my job it never did to dwell on such things, so I put it from my mind and left to drive to Reims to get ready for practice for the French Grand Prix.

LAT

CHAPTER 8
VANWALL VICTORIOUS, ALMOST

I still nursed my ambition to win Grands Prix in a car wearing British Racing Green, despite my wasted year in 1953. Although the season with Mercedes was a once-in-a-lifetime opportunity that I couldn't possibly have turned down, I felt my time with Maserati, however much I enjoyed the 250F, was merely deferring that ambition until I could find a British car that really could be a consistent winner.

In November 1955 I had a very instructive test day at Silverstone, trying out the three British Formula 1 contenders. The new BRM was a compact four-cylinder car that seemed to be as sensibly neat and simple as the V16 had been absurdly complex. The Connaught was slightly slower, and I felt that this gallant little team didn't really have the resources to produce an on-going front-runner. The Vanwall was comfortably the quickest of the three. However, after a couple of weeks of soul-searching, I announced that I would drive for Maserati in 1956.

But the Vanwall had certainly caught my attention. Tony Vandervell was a gruff, no-nonsense multi-millionaire who didn't suffer fools. He had inherited his father's engineering firm CAV and expanded it considerably, and also launched the Vandervell Products company to produce Thin Wall bearings. He was a patriot and a great motor racing enthusiast, having raced motorbikes and cars in his youth, and he was an early supporter of the BRM project. Then, infuriated by the delays and, as he saw it, gross incompetence surrounding the V16, he withdrew and fielded a succession of Ferrari single-seaters, painting them green and calling them Thin Wall Specials. The first true Vanwall Formula 1 car, using a four-cylinder engine based on a quartet of Norton motorcycle engines, appeared in 1954, and by 1956 he was fielding a very impressive looking machine, with a distinctive aerodynamic body shaped by Frank Costin and chassis input from Colin Chapman of Lotus.

Maserati decided to give the May Formula 1 Silverstone a miss, so I accepted Vandervell's offer of a one-off drive. Although this was a non-championship race it had a pretty full entry, with works Ferraris, BRMs and Connaughts, so this would give me a chance to see how good the Vanwall really was. The answer was, pretty good: I put it on pole position and Harry Schell in the other Vanwall was alongside me, faster than Fangio's Ferrari and Hawthorn's BRM. I won the race and set a new circuit record, jointly with Mike.

During 1956 Schell, who was Vanwall's season-long number one, frequently showed strongly, and at Reims he demonstrated the car's straight-line speed by coming up through the Ferraris to battle for the lead with Fangio. In doing so he passed my Maserati down the straight like I was standing still, so the combination of Costin aerodynamics and the tall, torquey, long-stroke, four-cylinder engine was obviously working well. I wanted to see how the Vanwall felt over a full race distance, so that October I tested two examples at Oulton Park, driving one for two and a half hours and the other for almost two hours. I presented Tony Vandervell with a long list of suggested improvements – and I signed for 1957.

During my first few races with Vanwall we learned various lessons and developed the car considerably. My team-mate was Tony Brooks, a brilliant driver whose achievements have never, I think, really received their due acknowledgment. Unfortunately we both had to miss the French Grand Prix: Tony crashed his Aston Martin badly at Le Mans, while I developed a serious sinus infection after a water-skiing accident that sent me to the London Clinic. The very rapid, very smooth Formula 3 graduate Stewart Lewis-Evans filled in at Rouen, and went well enough to be offered a permanent place as No 3 in our team.

The British Grand Prix at Aintree came next, and was a great vindication of all of Tony Vandervell's efforts. After my car went off-song I took over Brooks' and came back up the field to win my home race and score my first Grand Prix win for Vanwall.

After finding out in the German Grand Prix that the Vanwall was totally unsuited to the Nürburgring's bumps, we then had two great races in Italy. It was the only time the Pescara Grand Prix was a round of the World Championship, added hastily after both the Belgian and Dutch Grands Prix were cancelled because their organisers had money troubles. It was run over a superb 15.9-mile road circuit that suited the Vanwall's excellent handling – as long as you showed it who was boss – and its torquey power. Fangio out-qualified me in his 250F by quite a margin, but I got away ahead of him, behind Luigi Musso's Ferrari, and by lap 2 I was settled in the lead and stayed there to the flag.

Monza as a track could not have been more different, but I won the Italian Grand Prix three weeks later, again ahead of Fangio, and that left me second in the World Championship to the Old Man, who won his fifth and final title.

The Formula 1 rules were much changed for 1958, with the maximum permitted distance for a Grand Prix cut from 310 miles to 186 miles – something I regretted – and alcohol fuels banned. That required considerable changes to engine tuning, and Vanwall decided to miss the first Grand Prix in Argentina. That gave me a chance in something else, as I'll recount in a later chapter. Our first Vanwall win came at Zandvoort: I was the team's sole survivor, but I came home comfortably ahead of the BRMs of Schell and Jean Behra. At Spa I missed a gear on the first lap, a foolish mistake that blew my engine, but fortunately Tony won. At Reims I was

a smoky second to Mike, and at Silverstone my engine threw a rod. In Germany my magneto packed up while I was leading. I won in Portugal with Mike second, thanks to my defending him when the organisers wanted to disqualify him for push-starting his car against the traffic after a spin. At Monza my gearbox broke.

That left the final round in Morocco. I had won three rounds so far, Mike only one. But because of the Ferrari's reliability he had clocked up four more points than me. If I could win the race and earn the extra point for fastest lap, and if Mike finished third or below, I would be World Champion. Well, I did all I had to do: I won and I set fastest lap. The Vanwall didn't miss a beat. Late in the race Mike was running third, but in second place was his Ferrari team-mate Phil Hill, and of course the Ferrari pit signalled to Phil to slow so that Mike could move up to second place. Perfectly understandable team tactics, and I don't resent that at all. But of course I was bitterly disappointed: it was the closest I ever came to winning the World Championship, and I lost it by one point.

But what I always say now is this. Lots of people have won the World Championship once. That's not so special. I'm happy to be thought of as the best driver who never won the World Championship. Special pleading, maybe, but that's how I feel about it.

It wasn't all bad news. In 1958 there was a Constructors' Championship for the first time: with my points and Brooks' – because he also won three races that year – Vanwall were the winners, well ahead of Ferrari. It had been Tony Vandervell's dearest wish 'to beat those bloody red cars' and at the beginning of 1959 he announced that he was ending his full-time involvement in motor racing. So, in Formula 1 terms at least, I was on the move again.

↑ This was my one-off drive for Vanwall in 1956, at the May Silverstone. As the flag drops I'm not making a brilliant start from pole position, and Harry Schell beside me is even slower away. Fangio is getting the Ferrari going well, but on the right of the picture Mike Hawthorn is catapulting the BRM into the lead. Behind us are Peter Collins' Ferrari (2), Roy Salvadori's Gilby Engineering Maserati (15) and Archie Scott Brown's Connaught (5), with Bob Gerard's rather historic-looking Cooper-Bristol behind Archie.
◎ LAT

↗ This profile shot of the Vanwall shows how high the car was, because of its long-stroke engine and lofty valvegear, and the driver sitting on top of the bulky gearbox. But Frank Costin's elegant aerodynamics dealt with that very well. The Vanwall wasn't as forgiving to drive as the 250F, but even this early in its development it was a very effective racing car. After Mike dropped out when his BRM's timing gear broke, I won by over a lap and, jointly with Mike, set a new lap record.
◎ LAT

➡ Prize-giving on the start line at the end of the May Silverstone meeting. I'm at the microphone giving a few words of thanks to the Vanwall boys. Behind me is Jim Russell, who won the Formula 3 race. Roy Salvadori won both the small- and large-capacity sports-car races in Cooper and Aston Martin respectively, but evidently missed the prize-giving, because John Cooper and Aston Martin supremo David Brown are holding his trophies. Hidden behind John is Ivor Bueb, touring car victor in a Jaguar Mk VII, and the tall figure behind them is John Eason-Gibson of the BRDC. On the right is Archie Scott Brown, whose Lister-Maserati won the 2-litre category in the big sports-car race.
◎ LAT

↑ The 1957 Monaco Grand Prix was my first World Championship race for Vanwall, and it didn't turn out well for me. This is lap 1 at the old Gasworks Hairpin, three abreast with me on the outside of Fangio's 250F Maserati and Pete Collins' Ferrari. I went round the outside of Fangio to take the lead, and it was looking good until lap 3, when I came out of the tunnel down to the chicane, braked at my usual point, and found the front brakes weren't answering the pedal. With the rears locked up I skated helplessly into the wooden barriers, hitting them hard enough to break my nose on the steering wheel. Collins' Ferrari, which was just behind me, ploughed into the displaced barriers, and Hawthorn's Ferrari piled in on top of it. Fangio, typically, picked his way through the mêlée and went on to win the race, and Tony Brooks salvaged some Vanwall dignity by finishing second.

📷 *LAT*

➜ Because of a bad sinus infection, I only left hospital two days before going up to Liverpool for the British Grand Prix at Aintree. The previous month Tony Brooks had had an unpleasant accident at Le Mans when he turned his Aston Martin over at Arnage, and he was not fully recovered. We agreed that he was unlikely to be able to race the full distance and therefore, if anything happened to my car, he would hand over his to me. Nevertheless, in practice he was only 0.2sec slower than me, with Jean Behra's Maserati between us on the grid. Here is Behra making a brilliant start, while my Vanwall, with the white noseband, and Tony's get away side by side. Almost hidden behind Tony is Hawthorn's Ferrari, with Collins' Ferrari next up, and then a trio of Musso's Ferrari and the 250Fs of Schell and Fangio, with Stuart Lewis-Evans in the third Vanwall behind Fangio.

📷 *LAT*

➜ I got past Behra before the end of the first lap and pulled away into a good lead, and my mirrors were empty when after 20 laps my engine started to misfire. A quick pitstop, which dropped me to seventh, failed to cure it, so I came in again, and the signal was given to call Tony in.

📷 *LAT*

↑ It took 13 seconds for me to leap aboard Tony's car – because of his injured leg the mechanics had to lift him out – and when I took it back into the race on lap 27 the lap charts showed it was in ninth place. So I had some work to do. Here I am on the limit, taking the shortest route through one of Aintree's left-handers. Vanwall No 20 was going beautifully and I was seventh by lap 30, fourth on lap 46, and third on lap 69 behind Behra and Hawthorn. Then Behra's clutch fell apart, and Mike suffered a puncture, and with 20 laps to go I was back in the lead.

◎ LAT

↗ Tony bravely took over my car to try to get it back in the running, but the electrical problem persisted and eventually he brought it in to retire. The pain from his Le Mans injuries is clear from his face, with Tony Vandervell showing fatherly concern.

◎ LAT

→ With 11 laps left to run I was so far ahead of the rest of the field that I had time for a quick refuelling stop, just in case anyone had miscalculated on fuel consumption – I didn't want anything to threaten this crucial win. I jumped out and swigged a quick bottle of water while the lads sloshed in a couple of churns, and then clambered back in to drive to the flag. The Vanwall's high cockpit sides meant that the only way to get aboard was to use a back wheel as a springboard, but if you were going in from the left you had to watch out for the hot exhaust.

◎ LAT

⬆ It was a joyful moment when I took the flag with 26 seconds in hand over the Ferraris of Musso and Hawthorn. The statisticians were quick to point out that it was the first time a British driver had won a Grand Prix in a British car since Henry Segrave in 1923. As for me, after waiting so long to get myself into a truly competitive green car, it meant an awful lot to score my first win for Vanwall, in Britain.
📷 *LAT*

↑ I think our victory meant even more to Tony Vandervell as he held the British Grand Prix trophy aloft, to the cheers of the partisan crowd. When he was asked why he ploughed his fortune into building a British Grand Prix team he said, dismissively, 'Some people play golf; I play cars.' But for him it was a lot more serious than that: the honour of Great Britain was at stake, and he was determined to beat Ferrari and Maserati. Both Tony Brooks and I look in serious need of a hot bath, but very pleased with our day's work. Tony was quite rightly acknowledged as joint winner with me, because he had driven No 20 for its first 27 laps.
📷 *LAT*

↑ The Pescara Grand Prix used a simply wonderful road circuit that was just the sort of challenge I loved: almost 16 miles through narrow villages and up into the Abruzzi mountains, and then a long 175mph straight at sea level beside the Adriatic. It was the longest circuit ever used in the World Championship, rather like a mini-Mille Miglia for Grand Prix cars. Before the first day's practice, while the roads were still open and populated by bicycles, donkey carts and herds of cows, I did as many laps as I could in a Fiat 1100 to learn the place. Fangio was doing the same in a Lancia Aurelia, and I was none too happy when he took pole in his 250F Maserati a whole ten seconds faster than me. He and I were the only ones to break ten minutes. That still put me in the middle of the front row, and although Musso's Ferrari led the first lap, I was in front by lap 2. I had a worrying moment when my oil pressure began to fluctuate, but I had time for a pit stop to add oil and still run out the winner over three minutes clear of Fangio.

📷 *LAT*

⬆ Tony Vandervell could be a difficult man, but as long as his cars were winning he was happy. It was hot at Pescara, and it took me almost exactly three hours to complete 18 laps of that long track, which meant I'd averaged just under 96mph through village streets, the curves and dives in the mountains, and along the coast. No post-race podium nonsense and wasted champagne in those days: I'm holding a bottle of good honest San Pellegrino water.

📷 *Getty Images*

← The Italian Grand Prix crowds always expect red cars to fill the front row at Monza, but this was the heart-warming sight at the start of the 1957 race: all three Vanwalls up front. New boy Stuart Lewis-Evans took a brilliant pole position, 0.3sec ahead of me and 0.5sec from Tony. Rather obscured in the foreground, Fangio's 250F completes the four-car front row a further 0.2sec down; visible on the second row is Jean Behra's V12 Maserati.

📷 *LAT*

⬆ I took the lead at the start but the other two Vanwalls came with me, and we made up a battling quartet with Fangio. I managed to shake off the slipstreaming pursuit and, while Tony and Stuart both hit problems, for me everything went well, and when Fangio stopped to change tyres I was nearly a lap ahead of everybody. Just as at Aintree and Pescara, I made a late precautionary stop, fitting fresh rear tyres and taking on oil, and I still came home over 40 seconds clear of Fangio.
📷 *LAT*

⬇ Vanwall had won three of the four last Grands Prix of 1957, but the ever-consistent Fangio, with four victories, had won his fifth World Championship title. For the third year in succession, I was his runner-up. I always had boundless respect for Fangio, which after our year together at Mercedes became all the greater, and there was real affection between us. For me he will always be the greatest racing driver of my era, maybe of any era. Here we are, both filthy and sweaty, immediately after my win at Monza, with the lovely lady who was Juan's constant companion, and who was known to everybody in the Grand Prix circus as Fangina.

📷 *Getty Images*

← Four weeks after the 1957 Italian Grand Prix I married Katie Molson, a member of the Canadian brewing dynasty. Ken Gregory was my best man, and Mike Hawthorn and Peter Collins were ushers. I'd met Katie at Le Mans in 1956: I was in the pits with a pair of binoculars, scanning the crowd in the public enclosure on the other side of the road for crumpet, and I saw her. I waved to her to come over; she signalled back that she had no pass. I took off my driver's armband and waggled it at her, so she came over and I met her at the barrier into the pits. She was lovely, but to my regret and sadness we turned out to be incompatible. Our marriage was really at an end after barely a year, although officially we stayed together for three years because that was the legal minimum before divorce in those days. We remained friendly and we are still in touch.

📷 *Getty Images*

← Katie came to all the races and played her part in things: here I am scribbling in the little notebook she carried. Tony Brooks is in the background.

It can never have been easy being a wife or a girlfriend in the pits. Some of them would keep a team's lap chart (no electronic timing in those days) or carry out other background tasks. Others just looked decorative and tried not to get in the way.

📷 *Stirling Moss collection*

⬆ Monaco never seemed to be lucky for Vanwall. In 1958, with the cars running on pump fuel in accordance with the new regulations, I had problems in practice and could only qualify eighth. But I worked my up the field, round the twists and turns, and on lap 32 I took the lead from Hawthorn's Ferrari. A few laps later my Vanwall went onto three cylinders. Back at the pits a broken cam follower was diagnosed, and I was out. For the tight, lower-speed Monte Carlo street circuit we ran with shortened noses to avoid the possibility of damage in the racing traffic, which might close up the air intake and cause overheating. This also improved throughput to the radiator at Monaco's reduced speeds. Here I'm darting downhill from the Mirabeau Hotel to the railway station – both long gone now.
📷 *LAT*

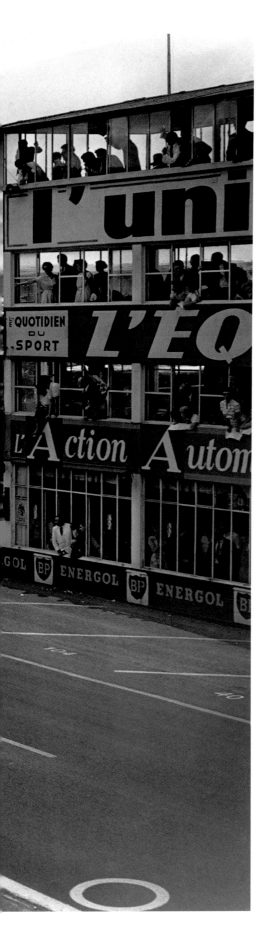

← Flat-out past the pits at Reims, chasing Fangio's Maserati and Harry Schell's BRM. After dropping a valve in practice my engine had been hastily rebuilt, but for safety I had to run a higher axle ratio to keep the revs down on this track's long straights. This handicapped me a fair bit, and Mike's Ferrari pretty much ran away with the race. He was chased by team-mate Luigi Musso until poor Musso crashed fatally. Fangio had a pitstop, Schell went out with a duff fuel pump, and I survived to finish a distant second to Mike. It wasn't a very satisfactory weekend.
🗗 *LAT*

⬇ None of us realised it, but Reims was Fangio's final Grand Prix. He had quietly decided to retire after this race, because Reims was the circuit where he had started his European career exactly 10 years before. He was now 47 years old. This shot shows what a good, tough battle we had in the early stages, fighting wheel-to-wheel for what became second place after Musso's accident. Then Juan had to stop for attention to his 250F's gear linkage, rejoining well down and coming back up the field to finish fourth. Mike, who had a comfortable 25 seconds on me by the end, came up to lap Fangio on the final lap, but lifted off and tucked in behind him so Fangio could run the full distance. That's an indication of the respect we all had for the Old Man.
🗗 *LAT*

← I took pole for the British Grand Prix and made a great start. Behind me here are Harry Schell's BRM and Roy Salvadori's Cooper squeezing Pete Collins' Ferrari, with Tony Brooks' Vanwall in pursuit. Hawthorn, who qualified on the outside of the front row, is on the extreme right of the picture, having apparently been caught napping by the starter's flag. But Collins was on absolutely untouchable form that day. He was in the lead by the time we came out of the first corner, Copse, and just ran away with the race.

📷 *LAT*

← I did my best to keep Collins in sight until, at one-third distance, my engine broke a con rod, and I clanked straight into the paddock to retire. Mike finished second, so this Silverstone race did nothing for my championship chances.

📷 *Klemantaski Collection*

↙ Not what it seems. Photographer Maurice Rowe, who worked for *The Motor* magazine, stationed himself at the apex of Becketts Corner with his ancient VN plate camera, and took a shot of my Vanwall and a shot of Mike's Ferrari from exactly the same spot. In those pre-computer days it needed a scalpel and a lot of care to join the shots together in this text-book demonstration of the difference between understeer and oversteer.

📷 *Maurice Rowe*

↓ Before Silverstone Mike and I had been running neck and neck in the World Championship, both on 23 points, and the press were making much of the battle between us two British drivers. In fact we continued to be friendly, as we had always been. Here, to the amusement of one of the Ferrari mechanics, we're indulging in a bit of horseplay, with Mike threatening me with a wheel hammer. The photographers behind are enjoying it as much as we are.

📷 *LAT*

↑ Lap 1 of the 1958 German Grand Prix at the Nürburgring. My Vanwall leads Tony's, then it's Schell's BRM, the Ferraris of Mike, Pete and Taffy von Trips, then Behra's BRM, Phil Hill's Ferrari and Roy Salvadori's Cooper.
📷 *LAT*

→ A classic shot that shows the true nature of the 14.2 miles of the Nürburgring. This is leaving the Karussel and aiming up the hill towards Höhe-Acht. No Armco barriers then, of course: just hedges, trees and a flimsy wooden fence. At the end of my first standing lap I was leading Mike by 6 seconds. On my second lap I broke the outright lap record with 9min 16.6sec, and on my third I brought it down to 9min 9.2sec. The car was perfect, and handling beautifully, and I was sure that as the fuel load lightened I would get under nine minutes. Then on my fourth lap, approaching the Schwalbenschwanz, the engine just switched off. Everything went silent. A tiny screw had come adrift in the magneto, and I had no more sparks. It was one of most enraging moments of my career. But this was nothing beside the news that Pete Collins, one of our close British gang of friends, had crashed fatally trying to catch Tony's Vanwall. There were quite a lot of fatal accidents in those days, and I had schooled myself to accept them as part of the game and move on. But Pete's death affected me far more than I would have wanted.
📷 *LAT*

⬆ The Portuguese Grand Prix circuit of Boavista ran around the harbour and up into the outskirts of Oporto, past houses, shops and lamp posts, over cobbles and even across tramlines, seen here as I lead team-mate Stuart Lewis-Evans. The Vanwalls now had a new nose intake to feed air to an enlarged oil cooler. I won this race, and Mike Hawthorn was coming home second when he spun on his last lap and stalled. On my slowing-down lap I saw him struggling to start the Ferrari by pushing it uphill. I drove slowly past him and shouted, 'Push it downhill!' So he did that, got the car started, and drove on to claim his second place. The stewards tried to disqualify him for going against the race direction, but I went to them in support of Mike and pointed out that he'd done this on the pavement, not actually on the track, and I persuaded them to reinstate him. It might not have helped my championship situation, but I felt it was the right and fair thing to do.

One other problem: late in the race, as I was cruising home, the Vanwall pit hung out a sign that I read as HAW REG, meaning Hawthorn Regular, to say he wasn't catching me. In fact it said HAW REC, meaning Hawthorn had set a new lap record. If I'd understood what the sign meant I know I could easily have pulled out the stops and gone quicker, and got that extra point for fastest lap. You could say that error of mine cost me the World Championship.

📷 *LAT*

➡ The championship battle then moved to Monza and the Italian Grand Prix. This shows what a great slipstreaming joust we had, with Mike and me both taking turns at leading. But then my gearbox started to play up, and finally it broke. It was my fifth mechanical failure in eight races – very frustrating. Tony won, Mike scored more points for finishing second, and this was all getting a bit too close for comfort.

📷 *LAT*

← We had to wait an agonising six weeks after Monza before the final round in Morocco. By now all the papers and magazines were full of the last-ditch fight between Mike and me. The mathematics said that, for me to be World Champion, I had to win in Morocco and set fastest lap, and Mike had to finish lower than third. At least I knew what I had to go out and do. I hope this doesn't sound conceited, but I did honestly feel in my heart of hearts that I was the natural successor to five-times champion Juan Manuel Fangio, having been three times his runner-up. And that season I'd had three wins – and a lot of unfortunate retirements – to Mike's one win.

📷 *Getty Images*

← Morocco's 4.7-mile Ain-Diab circuit consisted of a rough rectangle of public roads on the outskirts of Casablanca and was fast, with average speeds nudging 120mph. Mike took pole with me just 0.1sec slower, but this photo shows the rather different position just after the start, with me leading Phil Hill's Ferrari, then Jo Bonnier's BRM, Stuart's Vanwall, Mike's Ferrari, Tony's Vanwall and Behra's BRM.

📷 *LAT*

⬆ At speed in Morocco. The dented nose was caused by back-marker Wolfgang Seidel getting his Maserati in a muddle just as I was lapping him for the second time, and I watched my water temperature to see whether the damage had closed the air intake, but all was well. I led all the way, and set a new lap record: but it wasn't enough. Phil Hill ran second for most of the race, with Mike a long way back in third. But with 14 laps to go the inevitable signal went out from the Ferrari pit and Phil slowed right down to let Mike take the second place he needed. I won the race by nearly a minute and a half, he won the championship title by one point. My congratulations to Mike at the finish were genuinely meant, even though the long season hadn't turned out as I'd hoped.

Then I learned the worrying news that Stuart Lewis-Evans had been very badly burned. His engine seized and locked his rear wheels, and his Vanwall wrapped itself around a tree and caught fire. Tony Vandervell was distraught – it was the first time any driver had been seriously hurt in a Vanwall – and he flew Stuart home to get him into the Burns Unit at East Grinstead at once. It was in vain: he died six days later.

There was further tragedy the following January. Poor Mike had little chance to savour his World title, because he was killed in a car accident on the Guildford Bypass.

📷 *LAT*

CHAPTER 9
HELPING ASTON MARTIN TO BE CHAMPIONS

Throughout the 1950s the two great British manufacturers battling it out in sports car racing, from Le Mans to Goodwood, from Sebring to Oulton Park, were Jaguar and Aston Martin – the UK equivalent of the perennial Italian rivalry between Ferrari and Maserati. Ever since that first Tourist Trophy win in Ireland in 1950, Jaguar had been very important to me, right up to the end of the 1954 season. Then, with my move to Mercedes-Benz in 1955, the 300SLR became my sports car mount, and Mike Hawthorn joined Jaguar as their No 1. However, my 1956 deal with Maserati allowed me to race for other manufacturers when they didn't need me, and Aston Martin were happy to sign me on that basis.

That allowed me to do three British races for them, and three internationals, including Le Mans and Sebring. The millionaire industrialist David Brown, Aston Martin's owner, was a great enthusiast, while the team manager was John Wyer, a tough, stern-faced disciplinarian with a cynical sense of humour. I remember once in a long race, when he was told that one of our rivals had come to a halt out on the circuit, he fixed his informant with a beady eye and said, 'Nothing trivial, I hope?' If he wasn't happy with things he had a way of staring you down – the mechanics called him Death Ray. Working successively with Lofty England, Alfred Neubauer and then Wyer, I knew that racing teams operate much better under a tough boss.

My memory is that my Aston Martin signing-on fee was £50, but when I quoted this somewhere dear old John retorted that, unfortunately, he would never have got me for that. According to Aston's records, it seems that my 1956 retainer was £1750, and my six races with them that year earned me £3100, which I suppose was quite healthy in those days.

The Aston DB3S felt very different from the Jaguar D-type: with its smaller 3-litre engine it had appreciably less power and torque. But it felt compact and nimble – particularly after the Mercedes 300SLR that I'd been racing the previous season – and on twisty circuits it would usually have the legs of the Jaguar. My first outing was the Sebring 12 Hours, when I was paired with Peter Collins. We were comfortably out-qualified by the fastest Jaguars and Ferraris, but I made a demon getaway from the Le Mans-type start and soon got up to second behind Mike's Jaguar and ahead of Fangio's Ferrari. But that didn't last long: soon after I handed over to Pete the skew gears on the oil pump broke. A week later I was at the Goodwood Easter Monday meeting, and before the main race in the 250F Maser I did the 15-lap sports car race and had no trouble with that.

The sports car race at the May Silverstone was a bit hectic, but I managed to squeeze through a four-car pile-up on lap 1 to finish second to Roy Salvadori. Next came Rouen: Maserati decided rather late in the day to send works cars to the sports car Grand Prix there, by which time I'd contracted to do the race for Astons, so I was in the strange position of racing against my own team. But in the end neither of us won. The front row was Maserati/Ferrari/Maserati, and row 2 was Aston/Aston with Pete and me. With various retirements I found myself chasing Castellotti's Ferrari for the lead, but I couldn't quite do it: after 2 hours 10 minutes of racing, he took the flag 3.9 seconds in front.

Maserati didn't go to Le Mans, so I was paired with Pete again in a DB3S. I was determined to have another serious go at the race which, in 1955, Fangio and I would surely have won if the 300SLRs hadn't been withdrawn during the night. This time Pete and I chased the Ecurie Ecosse D-type of Ron Flockhart and Ninian Sanderson all the way, and even led them for chunks of the race, but finally we had to be content with second place.

Le Mans was never my favourite race. Using fewer revs and driving all the time below the car's limit wasn't how I liked to go racing.

But I have to say that Le Mans was never my favourite race. In those days the biggest task was trying to make your car last until the end, which meant using fewer revs and generally driving all the time below the car's limit, which wasn't how I liked to go motor racing. These days, when racing cars are fundamentally more reliable, all three drivers sharing a Le Mans entry are usually able to go absolutely flat out for the whole race, and that would have been much more my cup of tea.

In 1958, alongside my Vanwall commitments in Formula 1, I was a full-time member of the Aston Martin sports car team. To follow the DB3S, Aston had introduced a much-improved spaceframe car, the DBR1. It was a great machine in every way apart from its Achilles heel, the gearbox, which was clumsy to use and also broke frequently – a bit of an irony, this, as one of David Brown's most successful companies made gearboxes. In an effort to get on terms with the Ferraris and the Jaguar-engined lightweights like the Lister, there was a 3.9-litre version, the DBR2, which used a race-tuned version of the new engine developed for the DB4 road car. That was to be used in non-championship races, because the capacity limit for the World Sports Car Championship had now been reduced to 3-litres. That should have suited the DBR1 very well.

I had a couple of wins in British races at the Easter Monday Goodwood and the British Empire Trophy at Oulton Park. But I had a joyless time at Le Mans, leading for the first two hours before my engine blew, and in the Targa Florio I had various problems before the gearbox failed.

But two rounds of the World Sports Car Championship went really well for me. One of my most pleasing wins came in the Nürburgring 1000Kms. I shared with Jack Brabham but did most of the distance myself. The other was the Tourist Trophy. After the fatalities in the 1955 TT it was decreed that the Dundrod circuit should not be used for car racing any more, and the event lay fallow for a couple of years before being revived at Goodwood as a four-hour, two-driver race. Goodwood was very much Aston's back yard, and they swept the board, with Tony Brooks and me leading an Aston 1–2–3 ahead of Salvadori/Brabham and Shelby/Lewis-Evans.

In 1959 Aston Martin were determined to win Le Mans, and were prepared to sacrifice the rest of the season to concentrate on that one goal. But following my win in the previous year's Nürburgring 1000Kms, I persuaded them to send a single car and a couple of mechanics to that race. And Jack Fairman and I won it, not without considerable drama when, through no fault of his own, he went off the road. Then Astons did win Le Mans at last, although by taking my role as the team 'hare' seriously I was out with a blown engine after five hours.

That victory put them in with a shout of winning the World Sports Car Championship for Manufacturers. Ferrari were the favourites to win it, and it all came down to the final round, the TT at Goodwood. The full three-car works Aston team faced up to a full team of Ferrari Testa Rossas, but on that track, unlike Le Mans, we had the legs of them. Then our race was potentially ruined when our car caught fire in the pits and was almost burned out. But Roy Salvadori and I took over another team car and won the race – and Aston Martin beat Ferrari to the championship by two points.

Having won the title, and won Le Mans at last, Aston Martin then withdrew from top-level sports car racing at the end of 1959 to concentrate on their Formula 1 single-seater project, the DBR4. By the time it finally appeared, well into 1959, big, tall F1 cars that carried their engines in the front were becoming outmoded, and the DBR4 was never a success.

↑ The Aston Martin DB3S, with its flared front wheel arches and elegant crease running along the tops of the wings like a well-pressed pair of trousers, was a very pretty car. This is the Easter Monday Goodwood, and I'm going through the left-hander at St Mary's on my way to a comfortable win. The specialist sports car makers – HWM, Lister, Tojeiro and the rest – where just starting to make their presence felt in British races, and George Abecassis in the HWM-Jaguar beat all the D-types to take second place.

📷 LAT

⬇ The drivers for the sports car race at the 1956 May Silverstone walk along the track to take up their positions for the Le Mans start. From left: Archie Scott Brown, Jack Fairman with Reg Parnell behind him, Mike Hawthorn no doubt telling me a rude joke, Desmond Titterington on my left, then Pete Collins and, striding along all on his own on the right of the picture, Roy Salvadori.

Roy was always a charming fellow out of his car, but could be a hard bastard in it. That day he was driving his own DB3S, which for some reason proved a useful bit quicker than my works car. I led from the start but on the first lap Roy elbowed past me on the inside at Stowe. This edged me across onto the outside and, while I was sorting that out, the D-types of Des and Mike came by – whereupon Des spun, I thought because Roy had shut the door in his face. The spinning D-type was hit, hard, by Ninian Sanderson's D-type and the Astons of Pete and Reg. That produced four wrecked cars in the middle of the road, but Mike and I got through unscathed and I was able to pass Mike and chase Roy home.

I wasn't too happy about it all, and I told Wyer afterwards that I thought the chain reaction had been started by Roy. But I won the main race for Vanwall later that afternoon, so that cheered me up.

📷 *Getty Images*

← After the 1955 disaster the Le Mans circuit was radically remodelled. The pits were rebuilt further back, and a wide safety ditch separated the crowd – as dense as ever – from the track. This is the scene seconds after the Le Mans start, and I'm in Aston No 8, having already got away nicely. Mike Hawthorn's D-type is second, fractionally ahead of the Ecurie Ecosse D-type of Ron Flockhart, with Bob Walshaw's brave near-standard XK140 coupé looking very out of place. Next up are the D-types of Paul Frère and Jack Fairman, and Peter Walker's DB3S. The Frère and Fairman D-types crashed out of the race on the second lap, Hawthorn's D-type was delayed by a split oil pipe, and Walker crashed later. So the battle was between us and the Ecosse D-type.

📷 *LAT*

← My travel-stained DB3S, shared with Pete Collins, on Sunday morning. We had a race-long duel with the Flockhart/Sanderson D-type, and led the race during the rain on Saturday evening and again at dawn. But then we lost second gear and, although the car was still going very well in every other way, that was too much of a handicap and we had to settle for second place. So, I was second at Le Mans for the second time. I never won the damn thing.

📷 *LAT*

⬇ The clock says 4.20 on Sunday afternoon, and while we wait for our trophies the organisers seem to have laid on some very worthwhile crumpet to help us celebrate. From left are Pete, me, Ron Flockhart, Ninian Sanderson and, in overalls, Ecurie Ecosse chief mechanic Wilkie Wilkinson, next to Ecosse team patron David Murray.

📷 *LAT*

← The rain was so heavy before the 155-mile August Oulton Park sports car race that the organisers considered cancelling it, and the local fire brigade had to be called in to pump water off the track. Eventually they compromised by reducing the race distance to 110 miles. I rather enjoyed balancing the responsive DB3S in the conditions, and I led from start to finish. It was an Aston 1–2–3–4, with Brooks, Parnell and Salvadori following me home.

📷 *Stirling Moss collection*

← I signed for Aston Martin for all the races they contested in 1958, starting with the Sebring 12 Hours. This is the team relaxing before the race: Tony Brooks, Roy Salvadori, Reg Parnell, Carroll Shelby and me. John Wyer had now been appointed General Manager of Aston Martin Lagonda, so Reg hung up his crash helmet and stepped into the role of Team Manager. The DBR1, which had replaced the old DB3S, was a very nice car only let down by its dreadful gearbox, which managed to be both heavy to use and fragile. Tony and I led until we had a puncture, which dropped us behind Mike's Ferrari. I was making up the deficit, and had plenty of time left to do it, when the gearbox broke – not for the last time.

📷 *LAT*

⬆ I persuaded Aston Martin to send a car to the Targa Florio for Tony Brooks and me, but it was a wasted trip. Early in the race I managing to clout a rock and punctured a tyre. Cursing myself for my foolish mistake, I had to change the wheel by the side of the road. Then the crankshaft damper came away, giving me a ferocious vibration, and finally the wretched gearbox broke again. Before all that I managed to carve a big chunk off my own lap record, set two years before in the 300SLR – despite having a quick spin on that very lap!

📷 *Klemantaski Collection*

↑ A tense moment during the Nürburgring 1000Kms when my Aston, in the lead, and Mike Hawthorn's Ferrari, in second place, are in the pits at the same time. I'm just about to leave, having taken over from my team-mate Jack Brabham, while Mike, sharing with Taffy von Trips, is still out of the car helping with the refuelling while his rear tyres are changed.
📷 *LAT*

← Hustling the DBR1 along a typically undulating stretch of the wonderful Nürburgring. Jack Brabham didn't know the 'Ring very well then and his lap times weren't as quick as mine, and at one stage when he was in the car we lost the lead to the Ferrari. So I ended up doing 510 of the 625 miles. Although I was as fit then as I have ever been, almost six hours in the big Aston around the 'Ring was hard work, and I was completely shattered afterwards. But we beat the Ferrari by almost 4 minutes to win.
📷 *LAT*

⬆ The Tourist Trophy was revived at Goodwood in 1958. Ferrari gave the race a miss, and Jaguar were out of things now, although there were a couple of the very rapid Lister-Jaguars entered. Tony Brooks and I shared this DBR1, it was a sunny September day in Sussex, and everything went perfectly. We led home an Aston Martin 1–2– 3, with Salvadori/Brabham and Shelby/Lewis-Evans completing the trio, and I set a new sports car lap record. Job done.
📷 *LAT*

↑ In 1959 Aston Martin decided to devote all their efforts towards winning Le Mans, preparing three cars meticulously, and refusing to enter the Nürburgring 1000Kms because it was only two weeks earlier. But having shown the previous year what an effective weapon the DBR1 was around the 'Ring, I believed I could win it again. I pleaded with John Wyer to let me go, and in the end he agreed to send the team's spare car and two mechanics. All other expenses would be down to me, but I would keep any prize money earned. I wanted a steady, dependable co-driver to do the minimum to fulfil the two-driver rule, and I chose Jack Fairman.

I used to practise my Le Mans starts endlessly. I'd leave the car in first gear and jump in with my left leg already extended to hit the clutch, my right going straight onto the throttle, then punch the starter button and away. It worked well this time, and I was off up the road almost before anyone else had moved. By the time we streamed into the Südkehre I already had a useful advantage.

I had a 16-second lead at the end of the first lap, and after three hours I was five minutes in front. I came in to hand over to Jack for his short stint, and he was doing a good job out in front… when suddenly he was overdue. After a long pause Olivier Gendebien's works Ferrari came through in the lead, and news filtered through that car No 1 was in the ditch far away on the other side of the circuit. Desperately disappointed, I changed out of my overalls and packed my bag.

📷 *Getty Images*

⬇ Then a cry went up: 'Fairman's coming in!' I hastily pulled my overalls back on, and as Jack brought the car to a halt I almost dragged him out of the cockpit, jumped in and was back in the race. This was lap 23. I worked back through the field until I was third, behind the two fastest works Ferraris. On lap 28 I was second, and on lap 29 I had the lead back. After seven and a half unforgettable hours, we won by 41 seconds from Gendebien/Phil Hill.

What had happened was that a backmarker moved across on Jack, who managed to avoid the car but spun backwards into a ditch. In sheer desperation he managed to manhandle the car, all by himself, out of the ditch, heaving with his backside against the tail – which explained the additional dent. It was a remarkable effort, and he richly deserved to share in what I think was one of my most rewarding sports car victories.

📷 *LAT*

← The DBR1s' Le Mans preparation included semi-enclosed front wheels and rear spats for extra speed on the Mulsanne Straight, with a carefully moulded screen/tonneau and a slightly higher tail. The V12 Ferrari Testa Rossas were the cars we had to beat, and they were very quick that year, so it was going to be a tall order. John Wyer decided the way to do it was to use me as the hare, to raise the speed of the race and try to break the Ferraris. I was given a four-bearing engine, which developed more power than the seven-bearing unit because of reduced frictional losses, but at the possible expense of reliability.

And so it proved. I led for the first hour before Jean Behra's Ferrari went ahead. I clung on to him, and the other two works Ferraris were close behind. Meanwhile the other two Astons stuck firmly to their pre-arranged regular pace. At the end of two and a half hours, when I came in to hand over to Jack Fairman, we were still second, sandwiched by the two quickest Ferraris. Shortly before 9pm, when I'd just taken over for my second stint, the engine dropped a valve and we were out.

But we'd done the job: the Ferraris had been forced to run on the limit to race with us, and all three works cars were out by Sunday morning. So the remaining Astons finished a magnificent one–two, Salvadori/Shelby ahead of Trintignant/Frère. Aston Martin had achieved their goal of winning Le Mans at last, and it had been a good team effort.

📷 *LAT*

↓ Reg Parnell was now our fatherly team manager, and he used a loudhailer to make his instructions to the mechanics heard above the cars roaring past and the general hubbub. It's 6.30pm on Saturday, I've just brought in the No 4 Aston, holding second place behind the Behra/Gurney Ferrari, and I'm about to shout a few pointers in Jack Fairman's ear.

📷 *Stirling Moss collection*

← Having won the Nürburgring 1000Kms and Le Mans, Aston Martin suddenly found themselves in a position to steal the 1959 World Sports Car Championship from under Ferrari's nose. The final round was the Tourist Trophy at Goodwood, and we did it – but not without tremendous drama.

I was paired with Roy Salvadori, and we led the race until Roy brought the car in for fuel and tyres, and for me to take over for my second stint. John Wyer had complained to the Goodwood organisers before the race about their primitive refuelling hoses: they involved turning an on/off handle rather than having an arrangement that automatically shut off the fuel as soon as you let go of the handle, as on a conventional petrol pump. Apparently John told them: 'If we get through this race without a major fire, it'll be a miracle.' Well, we didn't, and the fire was ours. As the refuelling started some fuel was spilt, some of it splashed down onto the hot exhaust pipe, and the whole thing went up.

📷 *Getty Images*

⬇ Fortunately the fire was put out before the whole pits burned down, and meanwhile we had a race to win. At once the second-placed DBR1 of Carroll Shelby and Jack Fairman was brought in, and I took that over. By now the Bonnier/von Trips Porsche was leading: a much less powerful car, but its tyres lasted far longer than ours, so it needed fewer stops. I stayed in the No 2 Aston until the end, on the limit all the way, and in all I drove for four and a half of the six hours. Here I'm out of the car for a quick gulp of milk while the car gets more fuel and fresh rubber. We beat the Porsche by a lap – and Aston Martin beat Ferrari by two points to be crowned World Sports Car Champions.

📷 *LAT*

↑ The DBR1 was built from the start to win endurance races, and in the short sprint races on British circuits it wasn't usually as quick as the Lister-Jaguars and Cooper Monacos. In the sports car race supporting the 1959 May Silverstone I was in amongst them, with most of the leading being done by Roy Salvadori, in the John Coombs Maserati-powered Cooper Monaco, and Graham Hill's F1-engined Lotus 15. Graham retired with a chewed-up differential, and Roy won by 12 seconds from me.

📷 *Klemantaski Collection*

↗ I got my own back on Salvadori in the GT race the same day at Silverstone, when I gave the Aston Martin DB4GT its race début. This was a lighter, shorter-wheelbase version of the luxurious DB4, and it had no trouble outpacing Roy in John Coombs' Jaguar 3.4.

📷 *LAT*

➡ Before long the DB4GT Aston was being outpaced by the new 250GT short-wheelbase Ferraris, so a small batch was made with even lighter bodywork by Zagato. I was already a fan of the 250GT SWB, but I drove a Zagato Aston at the 1961 Easter Monday Goodwood and managed to put it on pole. Its handling was far from right, and not only did Mike Parkes beat me in the Maranello Concessionaires 250GT, but also Innes Ireland pipped me in John Ogier's 'normal' DB4GT.

    This is the start with me a bit slow away: alongside me are Parkes, Ireland and Graham Whitehead in his own 250GT, with Mike McKee's Lotus Elite coming up from the second row.

📷 *LAT*

CHAPTER 10
DARK BLUE WITH A WHITE BAND

In times gone by, in your passport you had to state your profession. Rob Walker's passport gave his profession as 'Gentleman'. That, almost better than anything else, summed up the man. He was invariably courteous and charming, he was tremendous fun to spend time with, and he loved a joke even if it was against him. Above all he believed that in motor racing the most important qualities were sportsmanship, honesty and a sense of fair play.

Even in the 1950s, when Grand Prix racing was light years away from the multi-million dollar TV show it is today, Rob's little band of dedicated enthusiasts, using what were usually last year's cars, couldn't be expected to beat the works teams. Yet they did. We won seven Grand Prix victories together, and his cars won twice more after I retired.

When Vanwall withdrew from Formula 1 at the end of the 1958 season, I had won 40 per cent of that year's Grands Prix and missed the World Championship by one point. I was probably in a position to get signed by virtually any works team I might choose, and if I'd done that I would no doubt have earned far more money. Yet, to the surprise of a lot of people, I signed for Rob. And I never regretted it. In fact, I would go so far as to say that if my 1962 accident hadn't ended my career, I would never have driven for anyone else in Formula 1 for as long as Rob had a car for me.

I say I signed for Rob, but in fact in all the five years I drove for him we never had a written contract. We trusted each other, and it would never occur to either of us to depart from what we had agreed between us on a handshake. I was never paid any retainer: Rob just gave me 60 per cent of whatever his car earned from each race in start money, prize money and trade bonuses. That was always our arrangement, 60/40, and it seemed fair to both of us.

Rob's stories were wonderful, delivered in his slow, plummy upper-class voice punctuated with his self-deprecating laugh. He was born into considerable family wealth, which originally came from Johnnie Walker scotch whisky. The house where he was brought up, Sutton Veny in Wiltshire, had 100 rooms, and from the age of 12 he was expected to dress for dinner and had his own valet to lay out his clothes. When he was 21 and still a Cambridge undergraduate he bought the ex-Bira racing Delahaye T135, and entered it for the 1939 Le Mans 24 Hours. He engaged an experienced racer, Ian Connell, to be his co-driver, the idea being that Connell would do the majority of the driving. But a leaking exhaust burned his feet and Rob had to drive the last 12 hours of the race single-handed. Remarkably, given his lack of experience, Rob went the distance, and finished eighth. He always believed it was important to dress correctly according to the time of day, so throughout the race he wore a dark pin-stripe suit at night and a Prince of Wales check during the day.

When he got married he promised his wife that he would give up racing, and instead he indulged his love of the sport by buying competitive cars for others to drive. Over the years he must have invested untold sums in his motor racing. He was no engineer, and didn't pretend to be: instead he had absolute faith in Alf Francis, who was his chief mechanic in all the time I drove for him. Of course Alf and I had gone through a lot together, going back to my HWM days in 1950. If I suggested any change of strategy or modification to the car, Rob would say, 'If it's all right with Alf, then it's fine with me.'

My first important race for Rob was the 1958 Argentine Grand Prix, which Vanwall missed because they had not yet

If my 1962 accident hadn't ended my career, I would never have driven for anyone else in Formula 1 for as long as Rob Walker had a car for me.

adapted their engines to run to the new pump fuel rules. The famous story of that race is retold overleaf, and it was the beginning of an extraordinary racing relationship. I drove Rob's cars, always painted in his racing colours of dark blue with the distinctive white band around the nose, in over 90 races between Argentina 1958 and Brussels 1962 – Formula 1, Formula 2 and GTs.

It would need a separate book to describe them all, but some of the highlights are shown on the next few pages. Several of them rank among the races I remember, out of my whole career, with the most pride: Argentina 1958 of course, Monaco 1961, Nürburgring 1961, and in a different way my two Goodwood TTs in the 250GT Ferraris. I finished third in the World Championship in 1959, '60 and '61. In 1959, even though we were seriously compromised by the unreliability of our Colotti gearboxes, I led more Grand Prix laps than anyone else, and was in with a chance of the title up to the final race. In 1960 I missed three of the nine rounds after my Spa accident, and in the new 1961 formula the Ferraris had the legs of all of us, although I was able to deal with them at Monaco and the Nürburgring.

It was at the United States Grand Prix at Riverside in 1960 that I had the only falling-out I ever experienced with Rob. I knew that the differential on our Lotus 18 was nearing the end of its life, and the night before the race we managed to get a new one out of Lotus. Alf was told to fit it in time for the race. But he reckoned there was nothing wrong with the old diff, and complained to Rob that fitting it would take all night, and would compromise the rest of his pre-race preparation. So Rob relented, and told him he didn't need to do it.

When I looked in on the garage around midnight and found out what was going on I was furious. I demanded of Rob how he expected me to win the race without the work being done, and stormed off back to my motel room. Then I had a think about it, and at 2am I slid a note under Rob's door saying: 'Whatever happens tomorrow, you know I will try my very utmost to win for you.' Next day, as I took the chequered flag to win the United States Grand Prix, Alf Francis was standing in the pit lane, holding the new diff aloft to make his point.

For 1962 Enzo Ferrari was very keen to get my services, but I told him I would only drive a Ferrari if it could be painted blue with a white band and be run by Rob Walker. Amazingly, after some discussion the Old Man agreed to this. A new Ferrari 156 was built up for me at Maranello, and I was all ready to spend my 1962 Formula 1 season in a blue Ferrari.

It was meant to arrive in time for the Easter Goodwood meeting, but it wasn't ready. So I drove the old Lotus 18/21 there. If the Ferrari had arrived, everything might have been very different…

Being part of Rob's small organisation meant that it concentrated more or less exclusively on my racing, and I could make a lot of the decisions and gather the team around me. Lotus boss Colin Chapman wanted to protect the interests of his own works team, so once we had our 18 he would never let us buy the later types: we always had to make do with one development level earlier. But I enjoyed being cast in the role of underdog. To beat the might of Ferrari as a privateer, or to show up Lotus with one of their previous year's cast-offs, always gave me great satisfaction.

I also think I had more fun with Rob than I would have done with any other team. Although it was a burning will to win that was the driving force behind all my racing, I didn't mind having some fun along the way.

⬆ I had a few special races in my career that stand out as being turning points. The 1958 Argentine Grand Prix was certainly one. Rob Walker's little 1960cc Cooper-Climax was far less powerful than the works Ferraris and Maseratis; but we calculated that, unlike them, it could run the full distance without a refuelling stop. But, in the heat, could the tyres last? Dunlop told us that they couldn't possibly, and we would have to change tyres mid-race. But the Cooper had four-stud wheels, as against the others' knock-off hubs, and any stop would lose a disastrous amount of time. So we decided to give it a go. It had to be a closely guarded secret, and I allowed myself to be heard around the paddock complaining: 'It's all right for them with their knock-off wheels. Our tyre changes are going to take us three minutes!'

Then, horsing around with Katie, she inadvertently poked me in the eye, scraping my cornea and blurring my vision. An Argentinian doctor prescribed eye drops and painkillers, and told me to wear an eye patch for several days. I did my best to conceal this lest the organisers should decide I wasn't fit to race.

Fangio's Maserati led from the start, and I kept in touch with the front-runners while already trying to preserve my rubber. Then my clutch failed, but I managed to drive on without it. Around half distance, one by one, the Ferraris and Maseratis stopped for tyres. To lull them all into a false sense of security Alf stood out in the road giving me an obtrusive lap-by-lap countdown to a stop, with a pile of fresh wheels ready in my pit. I kept going. I kept watch on my tyres, trying to read the front treads as I went through the slowest corners and my rears in my mirrors. I was using as little steering input as I could, letting the car run through the corners and feeding in the power gently to minimise tyre wear. I even went right off the track onto the grass on the inside of corners, as in this picture, because I thought grass would be easier on the tyres than tarmac.

Finally the Ferrari and Maserati pits twigged my ruse and urged on their drivers to go flat out to catch me. With Alf giving me the gap back to the Ferraris of Musso and Hawthorn, I tried to pace myself. I saw the tread on the tyres getting thinner and thinner, and then disappear so that they were completely smooth. Then a white strip of canvas – the casing of the tyre under the rubber – started to appear. As the gap on Alf's signals came down and down, the strip got wider and wider. Then the canvas started to grow whiskers, as it too started to break up.

As I took the chequered flag Musso was less than 3 seconds behind me, and my tyres would certainly not have lasted another lap. It was a historic day: the first ever win in a World Championship Grand Prix by a rear-engined car, and the start of a racing relationship with Robert Ramsay Campbell Walker that would last for the rest of my career.

📷 *Stirling Moss collection*

⬇ That Rob Walker was no engineer is evident here, looking bemused as he keeps his distance from the Cooper getting an engine change. The hoist is slung cheerfully from a beam in the roof. Rob was always happy to leave all decisions about race strategy – and even which races we should enter – to Alf and me.
📷 *Getty Images*

← From 1959, following Vanwall's withdrawal, I was driving for Rob full-time in Formula 1, and in Formula 2 as well. Monaco was the first round of that year's World Championship and our Cooper had a full 2½-litre Climax engine in an updated chassis, although I was still about 20bhp down on the Ferraris. But it was wonderfully nimble around the tight confines of Monaco, and here I am starting on pole alongside Jean Behra's Ferrari, which looks enormous next to my little car. Jack Brabham's works Cooper is on the outside of the front row; behind are the Ferraris of Tony Brooks and Phil Hill, Jo Bonnier's BRM and, coming through from the back, Bruce McLaren's Cooper. Note the extremely brave, or foolish, movie cameraman kneeling on the track on the right.

📷 *LAT*

↓ Once I had dealt with Behra and Brabham, I pulled away, very comfortable in my new Cooper and pulling out a lead of more than 40 seconds. Then, with just 20 laps to go, I felt a transmission vibration, and made a quick stop to see if it could be quickly fixed, but it couldn't. I rejoined, and half a lap later the gearbox disintegrated. Because we thought that the standard Citroën-based Cooper gearbox might not be strong enough for the full 2½-litre engine, we had commissioned our own special gearbox from Valerio Colotti in Italy. As the season went on, it was to prove a bad mistake.

📷 *Klemantaski Collection*

⬆ Three weeks after Monaco, it was the same story at Zandvoort. There was a great battle from the start, and it took me a while to get to the front, which I did with 15 laps to go. Three laps later, the wretched gearbox failed again. In the picture, with the enthusiastic Dutch spectators watching from the sand dunes, I have just got past Jean Behra's Ferrari, which had held me up for several laps. Coming into shot is Graham Hill's Lotus 16.
📷 *LAT*

➜ In 1958 Maria-Teresa de Filippis became the first woman to race in World Championship Grands Prix in her private Maserati 250F, although she only finished once, at Spa. Later that season she raced a Formula 2 Porsche that Jean Behra organised for her, but when he was killed at Avus in August she retired from the sport. These days she serves as honorary president of the Club des Anciens Pilotes de F1.

This photo was taken on the grid at the 1959 May Silverstone. Because it was a cool day, I actually wore that rather fetching cardie, complete with BRDC badge, in the race. I doubt if it was flameproof.

📷 *LAT*

← I knew the four-cylinder BRM engine was more powerful than the Climax, and we did try one in the back of a modified Rob Walker Cooper, but it didn't work very well. So Rob agreed that until we got our Colotti problems sorted out I could borrow a BRM P25.

Because I didn't trust BRM's race preparation, we arranged to run the car from the Highgate workshop of the British Racing Partnership, which had been set up by my father and Ken Gregory as an autonomous team. In charge there was Tony Robinson, who in 1953 had been my junior mechanic under Alf Francis when we were trying to make the Cooper-Altas work. This is the start of the French Grand Prix at Reims, with Tony Brooks and Jack Brabham neck and neck for the lead. Phil Hill's Ferrari is third, and my BRM, in BRP's pale green livery, is almost alongside Masten Gregory's Cooper.

📷 *LAT*

⬇ The Ferraris were very quick at Reims, with Tony out in front and Phil second, but despite having no clutch for most of the race I was gradually drawing Phil in. The heat was so great that the track was literally melting, and just after I'd set a new lap record in my chase I managed to spin on wet tar at the hairpin. Without a clutch, I couldn't prevent the car from stalling, so I seemed to be stuck. I put the car in gear and tried to push-start it, thinking that if I could get the engine to fire I'd jump aboard and catch it on the throttle. But of course this was a fruitless task, and in the heat I brought myself to near-collapse.

📷 *LAT*

← Two weeks later I did manage to get the BRM home in second place at the British Grand Prix at Aintree, but I was pleased to be back in the Cooper for the German Grand Prix, which that year was held on the extraordinary Avus circuit in the Western zone of Berlin. The steep, high-speed banking at one end, with no protection at the top, was made of brick, and the G-forces were such that suspension had to be packed up to prevent bottoming at speeds of around 160mph. The long, straight sections ran in both directions along a stretch of *autobahn*, and the whole place was a bit spooky.

The Ferraris were always going to be hard to beat here, but somehow I managed to qualify second between Tony Brooks and Dan Gurney. This shot shows us up on the banking on the opening lap, with Brooks' Ferrari leading me, the works Coopers of Masten Gregory and Jack Brabham, Bonnier's BRM and Gurney's Ferrari. Just one lap later I was out – despite Colotti's development work on the gearbox, it broke again. Most infuriating.
📷 *LAT*

← Rob ran a second Cooper for me to race in 1500cc form in Formula 2 events. For 1959 we introduced some variety into the Climax near-monopoly and used the German Borgward engine, with 16 valves and Bosch fuel injection, and it worked well: I won four races on the trot at Syracuse, Reims, Rouen and Clermont-Ferrand. But at the August Bank Holiday Monday Brands Hatch meeting the car was not handling at all well, and I had a spin that dropped me down the field. Working my way back I got stuck behind Jo Bonnier's works Porsche, and here I am doing my best to tell him that I'd quite like to get past, old boy. This is the notorious Paddock Bend, with its steeply falling apex, and we've both got our inside wheels clear of the ground.
📷 *LAT*

⬆ The Italian Grand Prix at Monza was something of a repeat of Argentina, because once again I decided that tyre wear was crucial, particularly of the left front. Jack Brabham had the idea of using a harder sports-car compound for that wheel only, and when we twigged what he had done we did the same, borrowing a tyre from a Lotus Elite driver who had crashed his car in a supporting race.

From the start I was happy to let Phil's Ferrari lead, with the other Ferraris of Dan Gurney and Cliff Allison just behind me. Sure enough, they all pitted for tyres at half distance, and I won quite comfortably from Phil and Jack.

That left the World Championship finely poised, with just the US Grand Prix at Sebring remaining. Tony Brooks, Jack and I all had a chance of winning the title. On lap 2 Tony was rammed by his team-mate Taffy von Trips, and on lap 5 my gearbox broke for the umpteenth time. Jack ran out of fuel on the last lap, pushed his car home to take fourth place – and was World Champion.

📷 *Klemantaski Collection*

↑ An interesting grid shot of British Formula 1 cars at the start of the 1959 Oulton Park Gold Cup. I'm on pole, while Jack Brabham, rear wheels spinning in a cloud of rubber smoke, gets well clear. Completing the front row are Chris Bristow's Yeoman Credit Cooper and the Lotus 16 of Graham Hill, who has his hand up to indicate to the chaps behind that he has stalled. Row 2 is Bruce McLaren's Cooper, Roy Salvadori's Cooper-Maserati and Tony Marsh's Cooper, which is swerving around the stranded Lotus. Row 3 is David Piper's Lotus and the Coopers of Stan Hart and Ian Raby, who has home-grown bodywork on his, with Arthur Owen (Cooper) and Paul Emery (Cooper-Connaught) at the back. After I had got past Brabham my pit signals told me that the stewards had penalised him a minute for jumping the start, so I eased off. Then the stewards changed their minds and removed his penalty, so, alerted by more pit signals, I had to press on and managed to beat Jack to the flag by 5 seconds.

📷 *LAT*

➜ The Syracuse Grand Prix in southern Sicily gave me my first taste of my 1960 Formula 2 mount: one of the new single-seater Porsches, turned out in Rob's colours but watched over by the factory. This is me on the opening lap leading Innes Ireland's Lotus, Taffy von Trips' Ferrari, Olivier Gendebien's Cooper and Jack Brabham's Cooper. Syracuse was what I call a proper circuit, with lots of hazards, natural and man-made, like the stone wall and the gateway in the picture. I set a new F2 lap record to go with the F1 lap record I already held. Then it started to rain and I found the Porsche was quite twitchy, and Taffy reduced my lead a bit. But things were still looking good for me when, just before half distance, the Porsche dropped a valve.

📷 *LAT*

➜ By contrast with Syracuse, the Austrian Formula 2 Grand Prix was held on the rather boring Zeltweg track, laid out around an airfield with straw bales making the corners. Here I am leading Hans Herrmann's works Porsche, Jack Brabham's Cooper and Tony Marsh's Lotus 18. This race ended in a Porsche 1–2–3, with me leading home Hans and Edgar Barth. The race was stopped three laps from the end because the excited Austrian crowd pushed down the barriers and invaded the track. Contrary to Porsche's reputation before and since, the reliability of their F2 car was disappointing, but in the end I did win four of my nine races with it, including the Aintree 200.

📷 *Stirling Moss collection*

← We started 1960 still Cooper-mounted in Formula 1, but at the Easter Monday Goodwood meeting I was trounced by Innes Ireland's new Lotus 18. Its shape may have been boxy and inelegant, but as I chased Innes I could see that it had superb balance through the fast corners and also put the power down very well, and there was simply nothing I could do about it. This shot, with just a smidgeon of opposite lock on, shows how hard I was trying, and I did set a new circuit record, but over the race distance the Lotus was slightly quicker. It was the same in the Formula 2 race, when Innes' 1500cc Lotus 18 outpaced my Porsche. The day after Goodwood Rob Walker got on to Colin Chapman and ordered an 18 for us.

📷 *Ferret Fotographics*

← Unfortunately our new Lotus hadn't arrived in time for the May Silverstone, and once again Innes showed the superiority of Chapman's thinking. It was wet throughout practice, and I blotted my copybook by shunting my Cooper badly enough to have to switch to our previous year's car. But in that I managed to earn pole by over 2 seconds, while Innes was only 11th fastest. But come the race, which was dry, it was all to no avail. I led from the start while Innes worked his way up the lap chart, then around half distance he went by and I just had to sit and watch. This shot shows how the low Lotus has suddenly made the Cooper look high and old-fashioned.

📷 *LAT*

⬆ The success of the Lotus 18 had confirmed Innes Ireland as a Formula 1 front-runner. Here Graham Hill, now leading the BRM team, has found something in the paper to amuse us.
📷 *LAT*

➜ My Lotus 18 arrived just seven days before the Monaco Grand Prix. In a quick shakedown at Goodwood I found it wonderfully responsive and quick, but much more delicate to drive than the Cooper, and less forgiving. I was to define it later like this: if you want to have fun, drive a Cooper; if you want to win races, drive a Lotus. Nevertheless, we took both cars to Monaco, and I tried both in practice before deciding to race the Lotus, which I put on pole, 1 second quicker than Brabham.

My start wasn't great, and this shot as the field shuffles round the Gasworks Hairpin after the start shows Jo Bonnier's new rear-engined BRM leading from the second row: I think he was already moving when the flag fell. Behind him are Jack Brabham's Cooper, the Yeoman Credit Coopers of Tony Brooks and Chris Bristow, my Lotus, Innes Ireland's Lotus and Phil Hill's Ferrari.

📷 *LAT*

It took me 17 laps to get myself into the lead, and I stayed there until it started to rain heavily. Having never driven the Lotus in the wet I took my time to see how it felt, and Brabham went ahead – only to lose the lot at Ste Devote, right in front of me. I missed him by millimetres just before he hit the wall. By half-distance my lead was back up to 14 seconds over Bonnier – when my engine suddenly went onto three cylinders. My heart sank and I stopped at the pits, but Alf replaced a loose plug lead and out I went again to chase Bonnier. I retook the lead and held it to the end, to win my first race in a Lotus, and score Lotus' first Grand Prix victory. Afterwards Alf found that two engine mounts had broken, and the front of the engine was hanging on by a water hose. It underlined the Lotus reputation: fast, but fragile.

📷 *Klemantaski Collection*

⬆ As the British national anthem is played, I stand to attention in the royal box with Princess Grace and Prince Rainier. I am not a sentimental man, but I must confess to feeling at this moment the old pricking behind the eyelids.
📷 *LAT*

← In the Dutch Grand Prix a week later I could not repeat my Monaco success, but I had a good race. Here I'm leading the field through Tarzan Corner on lap 1, followed by the works Lotuses of Innes and Alan Stacey, Phil Hill's wildly understeering Ferrari, Jo Bonnier's BRM and a slow-starting Jack Brabham. Somehow Jack was in the lead by the end of lap 1, so I sat behind him, confident that I could find a way past before long. But after 17 laps his wheels threw up a heavy chunk of kerbing that smashed into my left front wheel, puncturing the tyre and bending the rim. I managed to hold the car straight and lurched back to the pits, where it took a very long time for Alf & Co to change the wheel, struggling with the Lotus' six wheel nuts. When I rejoined I was down in 12th place, and I had to drive on the limit to convert that to fourth place by the end.

📷 *LAT*

⬇ I was very happy with the speed and the competitiveness of the Lotus, but at the next Grand Prix, on the very fast Spa-Francorchamps road circuit in Belgium, it all went very wrong. During Saturday practice I was going for pole when, slicing through the long, fast right-hander at Burnenville at about 140mph in fifth, my left rear wheel came off. At once I planted my foot on the brake as the car spun down the road like a top, but it must still have been doing nearly 100mph when it hit the bank. I was thrown out of the car, and the next thing I knew I was on my hands and knees on the grass verge, unable to breathe. My car ended up a further 100 yards down the road. Bruce McLaren stopped and came to my aid, other drivers stopped too, and finally an ambulance arrived. I was flown back to London the next day with broken legs, crushed vertebrae in my back, a broken nose, two black eyes and other injuries. It was by far the worst accident I'd had.

It was a dreadful weekend because during the race two British drivers died, both of them very quick rising talents. Chris Bristow tangled with Willy Mairesse when they were fighting over sixth place, and he went through a barbed wire fence about 10 feet from the road and was decapitated. Alan Stacey died because of a cruel fluke: he was hit in the face by a bird, which stunned him, and he went off the road and was killed instantly. Both incidents happened right where I had crashed the day before, at Burnenville.

The picture shows the remains of my Lotus being inspected by Belgian journalist and racer Paul Frère.

📷 *Stirling Moss collection*

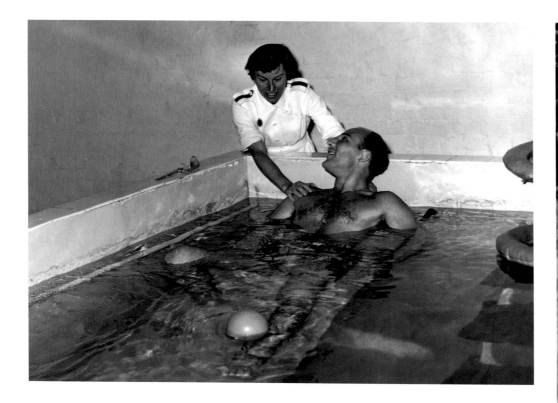

↑ Being injured in an accident in the middle of a busy season is bad news, but I was determined to recover as quickly as possible. The people at St Thomas' Hospital in Lambeth were wonderful, and my treatment included the hydrotherapy shown here. Within four weeks I was able to walk without sticks, and I was discharged 31 days after the crash. Six days after that I was at Silverstone testing my new Lotus 19 sports-racing car, and seven weeks after the crash I raced it in Sweden, at Karlskoga, and won.
📷 *Stirling Moss collection*

➜ My comeback Grand Prix was the Portuguese race at Oporto. I was disputing the lead with John Surtees, who'd just moved across from bikes and was having his third-ever Grand Prix in a works Lotus 18, when my engine went off-song, and I had to make two pitstops for fresh plugs. Then, with just four laps to go, I spun when a front brake locked. I got the car restarted by pushing it downhill against the traffic, just as I had advised Mike Hawthorn to do two years before when we were disputing the championship, and I was disqualified. There was no witness to speak up for me as I had for Mike, and my own appeals for reinstatement failed – but never mind, we were only talking about fifth place.
📷 *LAT*

⬆ For the first time there was a round of the World Championship on the USA's West Coast, at Riverside. It was the final round of the year, and although I was well out of the running for the title – Jack Brabham had already clinched that in Portugal – it was very satisfying to score a comfortable win ahead of Innes' Lotus 18 and Bruce McLaren's Cooper. In fact even in my truncated season I was able to finish third in the series, which was pleasing.

At the party after the race somebody presented me with a cake, a beautifully made representation of a Lotus 18 complete with marzipan and coloured icing. Remembering Spa, I broke off the left real wheel and offered it to Colin Chapman. He didn't think that was at all funny.

📷 *LAT*

➔ For the 1961 season the Formula 1 regulations changed dramatically, with engine sizes coming down to 1500cc. This was unpopular among some promoters in Britain and Australia, so the grandly named Intercontinental Formula was instituted, effectively catering for the 1960-style F1 cars, while down-under they had their own Tasman Formula with a 2.7-litre limit. The Intercontinental Formula didn't last very long, but so I could run in that as well Rob bought the latest Cooper 'low-line' model, seen here in the Silverstone pits, fitted with a 2½-litre Climax. I did four Intercontinental races that season, won three of them and retired from the other when leading due to a transmission breakage.

📷 *Stirling Moss collection*

➔ The May Silverstone International Trophy was torrentially wet, but my Intercontinental Cooper worked wonderfully well in the conditions, balanced and predictable. I really enjoyed this Grand Prix-length race, which had a strong field including World Champion Jack Brabham, John Surtees, Jim Clark, Graham Hill, Tony Brooks and Innes Ireland. Bruce McLaren beat me to pole by 0.6sec, but once I'd got into the lead I just settled down to appreciate it. By the end I had lapped the whole field.

📷 *Stirling Moss collection*

⬆ The latest Lotus, the 21, appeared for the Monaco Grand Prix in the hands of Jimmy Clark. As privateers, it was not made available to us, so I had to be happy with my 18. But I put it on pole ahead of Ritchie Ginther's Ferrari and Clark. As we lined up for the start, drama: I noticed that a chassis tube was cracked. Without fuss Alf calmly wheeled the Lotus away from the other cars on the grid, got his welding gear from the truck and welded it up. The flame of his torch was inches away from 40 gallons of fuel, although he took the token precaution of draping wet cloths over the accessible areas of the tanks.

This picture is lap 2, going up the hill towards Casino Square. Ginther is already out of shot and Jimmy is leading me and the Porsches of Dan Gurney and Jo Bonnier. Clark made an early pit stop, Phil Hill moved his Ferrari up to third, and I caught and passed Ginther to lead by lap 14. From then on my job was to keep reeling off the laps as fast and as consistently as possibly, under constant pressure from the Ferraris. They had about 30bhp more than my Lotus, and for most of the race were running close together less than 4 seconds behind me.
📷 *LAT*

⬅ The weather was extremely hot at Monaco, so to reduce cockpit temperature we simply removed the 18's side panels. The car performed perfectly, and in the end I won the race by 3.6 seconds. It was a race I like to think of as one of my very best, and it was certainly one when I hadn't been able to relax for a single second: every lap had to be flat out. What made me particularly chuffed was a little sum I did afterwards. My pole position qualifying time was 1m 39.1s. My race time, for 100 laps, was 2hrs 45mins 50.1sec. That means that for every one of my 100 laps, even with the standing start, I averaged just 0.4sec more than my pole time. Or, putting it another way, if I had done every single lap at my pole speed, I would only have improved on my race time by 40 seconds. I was quite pleased with that.
📷 *LAT*

← During 1961, that first year of the 1500cc Formula 1, the shark-nose Ferraris had the legs of all of us and were generally the quickest cars in the field. Until Watkins Glen – Innes Ireland's only Grand Prix victory – they won every World Championship round but two, when I was able to beat them on the twistiest circuits, Monaco and the Nürburgring. Here in the Dutch Grand Prix at Zandvoort I'm leading Ritchie Ginther's Ferrari, which I did beat into fourth place. But the other Ferraris of Taffy von Trips and Phil Hill finished 1–2.

Third was Jimmy Clark in a Lotus 21, and after that race Rob's little team started the process of updating my Lotus 18 to partial 1961 specification, with slimmer body and modified rear suspension. But we couldn't get our hands on a full-spec 21. That was the disadvantage of being a privateer: the works teams only ever wanted to sell us last year's car.

📷 *Klemantaski Collection*

↑ In 1961 Formula 1 drivers were a friendly little gang – so different from today's aloof superstars. In this motley group before the German Grand Prix are, from left, Jim Clark, John Cooper, Innes Ireland telling a joke as usual, Jack Brabham, me, Graham Hill looking stern and Jo Bonnier looking nonchalant (with Porsche team boss Huschke von Hanstein behind them), then Bruce McLaren and lofty Dan Gurney. Sadly Jimmy, Jo and Bruce were all destined to die in racing cars, Graham at the controls of his aeroplane.
📷 LAT

← I always loved the challenge of the old Nürburgring, 14.2 miles around, 172 corners, and no more protection than you'd get on any rural road through hilly, wooded countryside. I knew it was my best chance to beat the Ferraris, but another challenge came from Jack Brabham, who had the new V8 Climax engine in his Cooper against all of our Climax fours. I decided to use Dunlop's new soft-compound tyre, identified by a green spot on the sidewall. When I told the Dunlop guys I was going to use Green Spots and intended to go the full distance on them, they refused to take any responsibility, and said I would almost inevitably suffer a high-speed tyre failure. I decided that if we were to have any chance of beating the Ferraris we had to take that risk. I got Alf to paint the green spots black, so nobody else would realise what we were up to.

As the race settled down it was me holding off the Ferraris again, this time Phil and Taffy. They were putting me under real pressure and I was on the absolute limit in my Lotus, getting airborne over the humps and looking for split seconds anywhere I could around that long track that I knew so well. And all the time I was wondering how long my tyres would last…
📷 LAT

← Then, to my great good fortune, it started to rain: not heavily, but enough to make the track quite damp and slippery. That both cooled my tyres and lessened the Ferraris' power advantage. I was able to keep my buffer back to the red cars, and took the flag 21 seconds ahead of them. It was a very pleasing win on a circuit I loved, and I had no idea that it would be my last championship Grand Prix victory.

📷 *LAT*

⬇ That German weekend was a bit hectic, because several of us were also doing the Brands Hatch Intercontinental race the next day, Bank Holiday Monday. A Wednesday practice session had been laid on for us at Brands, then we rushed to the 'Ring on Thursday for Friday and Saturday practice, did the Grand Prix on Sunday and somehow got back to Brands for Monday. John Surtees, still in only his second Grand Prix season, was very much part of the Formula 1 circus now. At Brands his Yeoman Credit Cooper led my Cooper for the first 20 laps until he spun at Clearways and clouted the bank. Three laps later my gearbox went, leaving the race to Jack Brabham.

Most of us had flown back from Germany the previous evening on one of John Webb's Webbair charter flights, but Jimmy Clark and Colin Chapman were brave enough to fly back with Innes Ireland in Innes' own light aircraft. It had been a long day, and somewhere over France, one by one, they dozed off. Suddenly they all woke with a start, and Innes said, 'Who's doing the driving?' Jimmy said, 'We thought you were!' For about 10 minutes the plane had been flying along by itself…

📷 *Stirling Moss collection*

↑ Something really different was the Ferguson P99, a front-engined single-seater built to evaluate the four-wheel-drive system being developed by Ferguson Research. They passed it to Rob Walker to run, and it was painted in his usual dark blue with a white noseband. I drove it for a few laps in the British Grand Prix after my Lotus had broken, and in pouring rain I was amazed by its traction and braking, although it required a very different driving style, understeering strongly. It had originally been designed to take a 2½-litre Climax engine, and the extra weight of its complex transmission was a penalty when it ran in 1½-litre form, but in wet conditions it was brilliant.

So in September 1961 we entered it for the Oulton Park Gold Cup. This non-championship Formula 1 race boasted a fine field with Brabham, Clark, Surtees, Hill, Brooks and the rest, but I was lucky that the track was damp, although not actually wet. I made a slow start in second gear because first would not engage, but by lap 6 I was leading. As the track dried I set a new F1 lap record, and came home 45 seconds ahead of Brabham. I would have loved to have spent more time working with this fascinating car, but sadly I never drove it again.

📷 LAT

→ After the World Championship season was over, we used to keep busy over the winter with races in South Africa (the Springbok series) and in Australia and New Zealand (the Tasman series). In 1961, in both the South African Grand Prix at East London on Boxing Day and the Natal Grand Prix the week before at Westmead, my Lotus 18/21 was beaten by Jim Clark's works Lotus 21. This served to remind me how the 21, with its inboard front suspension and canted engine reducing its frontal area, really did have the edge on my hybrid 18/21 – and also that Jim Clark was developing into a superb driver. At East London I wasn't helped by the fact that I was quite unwell, and had had no sleep the night before. Here is Jim getting the laurels and the trophy, while I'm looking slightly secondhand.

 *Stirling Moss collection*

→ In the Tasman series things went much better. At last I had a Lotus 21 – because for 1962 Lotus themselves were moving on to the 24, and then the monocoque 25. Rob had it fitted with a 2½-litre Climax to run in the Tasman series, and we took my Intercontinental Cooper as well. I won the New Zealand Grand Prix at Ardmore in some of the heaviest rain I can remember. The track was awash, and at two-thirds distance the organisers decided to hang out the chequered flag, at which point I was running 1 minute 40 seconds clear of John Surtees' Cooper. This shot was taken a week later during the Lady Wigram Trophy at Christchurch, where it was dry and hot. But I still decided I could make the Green Spots last the 150-mile distance. They did, just – the rears were bald by the end, and the fronts little better. I led from start to finish, and Jack Brabham finished second ahead of John Surtees.

Terry Marshall

⬆ The Brussels Grand Prix on 1 April 1962 was run in two heats. Alf and the boys had managed to shoehorn one of the new Climax V8s into the old Lotus 18/21: I wasn't particularly happy with the result, but I was able to get within 0.2sec of Jimmy's new Lotus 24 in practice. I made a demon start but then locked up my brakes going into the first corner and shot up the escape road. By the time I'd found reverse gear and got back onto the track the rest of the field had gone. I worked my way back up to second place in that heat, finishing 5.5sec behind Graham Hill's BRM. Here I'm following Willy Mairesse's sharknose Ferrari in Heat 2, with Surtees' Lola in third place.
📷 *LAT*

⬅ Mairesse went off, Surtees' engine failed, and I was left with a nice lead. I set a new outright lap record, and then after only 11 laps of that second heat my timing gears disintegrated. Although I had no way of knowing it, that was the end of my last ever race in the Rob Walker colours, which I had carried since early 1958.
📷 *LAT*

⬆ Underlining the fact that Formula 1 in those days was just like one happy family, when Graham Hill's baby son was christened he threw a party in his North London home. Here is young Damon Graham Devereux Hill at the wheel of his first car, admired by Bruce McLaren, me, Tony Brooks, proud father Graham, Jo Bonnier, Huschke von Hanstein and Taffy von Trips. Thirty-six years later that little chap would become the first son of a World Champion to win the World Championship.
📷 *Getty Images*

⬅ The Ferrari 250GT short-wheelbase was one of those magical cars in which the vital ingredients – engine, chassis, beautiful body – all seemed to be perfectly aligned. In 1960 the TT, which I'd won three times at Dundrod and twice at Goodwood, became a three-hour, one-driver race for Grand Touring cars. Dick Wilkins had a 250GT SWB and was happy to lend it for the race to Rob, who of course had it sprayed in dark blue with a white noseband. My closest challengers were the Aston Martin DB4GTs of Roy Salvadori and Innes Ireland, but once we had gone through our tyre changes I was able to run home a comfortable winner by two laps. To underline that the Ferrari was a proper road-going Grand Touring car, it was fitted with a radio, and I was able to listen to the BBC Light Programme and the live race commentary from Raymond Baxter and Robin Richards, giving me my gap back to the Astons.
📷 *LAT*

← In the 1961 TT I had to work a bit harder. Dick Wilkins and Rob had bought one of the new Competizione 250GTs, which looked just the same but were lighter and had a bit more power. Mike Parkes had an identical bright red car, run by the British Ferrari importer, Colonel Ronnie Hoare of Maranello Concessionaires. Mike drove extremely well: he led from the start and, although I got past on lap 8, he continued to sit on my tail. After we'd had our first tyre stops he caught up with me once more, setting a new GT lap record in the process, but this punished his tyres and he had to stop again for another set. That allowed me to ease away to win by over a lap, but Mike still finished second ahead of the Aston Martins of Roy Salvadori, Jim Clark and Innes Ireland. During my pitstop Dunlop's man examines the wear on one of the used tyres, the first churn of fuel is going in and I'm out of the car ready to heave the next one over.

📷 sutton-images.com

⬇ Job done, Rob and I hold the famous Tourist Trophy. It was the seventh time I had won it. It was my inestimable good fortune to drive for Rob Walker for as long as I did. We went through many adventures and excitements, and whatever was happening on or off the track he never lost his ever-supportive, gentlemanly approach to our motor racing. He was a wonderful friend.

📷 LAT

CHAPTER 11
SUPPORTING CAST

As I've said before, all I ever wanted to do was race cars, at every possible opportunity. Anything to avoid an empty weekend. Early in my career I'd say, 'Give me £50 and a share of the prize money', and I'd race anything. Later on my rates may have gone up somewhat, but if I wasn't committed to another car or another race, I'd be happy to get my bum into whatever was going. And it didn't have to be a Ferrari or a Maserati – although I preferred it if it was something I thought I could turn into a winner. It wasn't just for the money: it was because I loved racing. I always hoped that if anyone had a car that needed a driver, their first thought would be, 'Let's see if Moss is free.'

As a result I turned up in some surprising vehicles. You wouldn't expect a Grand Prix driver to race an Austin-Healey Sprite, but I did because it was fun – especially as my team-mates were Innes Ireland, Pedro Rodriguez and Steve McQueen. This was in 1962 for a three-hour 1-litre GT race at Sebring, the day before the 12 Hours. Steve was a good guy: he fitted in well with the team and he wasn't a bad driver either. It was the third time my friend Donald Healey had persuaded me to do this race – in 1960 and '61 it was run over four hours – and it always got me nicely played in for the serious business of the 12 Hours the next day. But I never managed to beat the 1-litre Abarths, which were much more serious bits of kit.

Of all the sports racers I drove, there are two that stand out. One was the Birdcage Maserati, so called because its chassis was made up of a latticework of tiny-diameter tubes, all meticulously triangulated to produce a rigid structure of low weight. It had excellent Dunlop disc brakes, and inelegant but functional bodywork made up of simple, skimpy aluminium panels. With a straight-forward torquey four-cylinder engine it was a very effective race car.

Unfortunately when Maserati produced it they were in the middle of a financial collapse and couldn't afford to run the cars themselves, so they sold a couple to an American called Lucky Casner whose Camoradi team ran them with backing from Goodyear. They weren't very well organised, but I won the Cuban Grand Prix, and the Nürburgring 1000Kms with Dan Gurney. That was my fourth win in the 'Ring 1000Kms, against pretty long odds because we had a lengthy stop to repair a broken oil pipe, and it remains one of the sports car victories I remember with most satisfaction.

Maserati then produced the prototype for a rear-engined version, which in theory should have been even better, but they didn't have the funds to develop it properly. In its later form it had a V12 engine, a development of the V12 that was run in the 250F in 1957, but I never drove that.

The other car I really liked was the Porsche Spyder. I reckoned that, despite its little flat-four air-cooled engine and lowly power output, it was light enough and handled well enough to win the Targa Florio and the Nürburgring 1000Kms. I very nearly won the former, until the car broke five miles from the finish, while at the 'Ring I found we needed wet, slippery conditions to beat the big Ferraris. That's what Graham Hill and I got in the 1961 race, and with several of the other cars running into trouble we were well-placed for a win – and then the engine blew up.

Until I had my 1962 accident I was all set to become a Ferrari Formula 1 driver, wearing Rob Walker's blue colours, and there probably would also have been pale green sports and GT Ferraris under the UDT-Laystall banner. But strangely the first time I raced a Ferrari wasn't until December 1957, when I won the Nassau Trophy in a borrowed 290S. Three months later I did the Cuban Grand Prix in a 4.1-litre 335S entered by NART.

It was immediately obvious that they were kidnappers. Fangio said, 'Don't take him, take me.' It was a typical Fangio gesture.

The North American Racing Team was run by the US Ferrari importer Luigi Chinetti, who was close to the factory and could usually get his hands on the latest *tipi*.

The story of that Cuban race bears telling in some detail. As at the previous year's event, when I drove Maseratis, the Batista regime was still in power, but now Fidel Castro's communist rebels were hiding in the hills. The track went around the city of Havana, with huge crowds and very little spectator control, and the organisation was completely chaotic: practice started four hours late. Fangio took pole in Jim Kimberley's Maserati 300S, and my NART Ferrari was second quickest.

The drivers were all staying in the smart downtown Hotel Lincoln. The night before the race Fangio, Katie and I were in the lobby about to go out to dinner when two men sidled up to us with their hands obtrusively bulging in their pockets, and one of them said to me: 'You must come with us.' It was immediately obvious that they were kidnappers, and at once Fangio said, 'Don't take him. They are on their honeymoon' (which of course we weren't) 'and his wife will be frightened. Take me.' It was a typical Fangio gesture. They bundled him out into a waiting car and drove off.

Fangio told me later that they took him to their hideout, looked after him courteously, fed him, and gave him a radio so that he could listen to the live broadcast of the race. After it was over the Argentine Embassy in Havana was told where he was, and embassy staff went to fetch him, by which time the rebels had disappeared back into the hills. Their aim was to get publicity for their cause, and they certainly succeeded, for the kidnap of the motor racing World Champion made headlines around the globe.

The race itself was just as surreal. From the start I battled for the lead with Masten Gregory in John Edgar's 4.9-litre Ferrari on a track that quickly became very slippery because Roberto Mières' Porsche had split an oil line and sprayed lubricant around the entire lap. After only six laps a local guy, Armando García Cifuentes, slid off the road in his 2-litre Ferrari and into the crowd, killing seven people and injuring dozens more. Masten was leading me at this point, and various people were frantically waving red flags all round the track. But I knew the rules: a red flag to stop the race can only be shown at the start/finish line. So I changed down into second, accelerated past Masten, crossed the finish line and stopped. I was declared the winner, and Masten was absolutely furious. I told him that I had done nothing wrong, I'd simply read the rule book. He said he'd protest, and I said, 'Don't do that, if they disqualify me that'll give them an excuse not to pay one of us any money. Let's pool our winnings for first and second, and split it.' So that's what we did.

Surprisingly I did go back to Cuba for the 1960 race, and that gave me my first win in a Camoradi Birdcage Maser. By that time Batista had been overthrown and Castro was in power. After that the race was no longer held: no doubt the communist regime felt that motor racing was far too bourgeois.

I raced various other unlikely machines, from Brian Naylor's one-off JBW-Maserati – Brian lent it to me to win two heats at a Roskilde meeting after my Maserati's engine broke – to a later-type Sunbeam Alpine, which Rootes asked me to drive at Riverside with Jack Brabham in 1961. It was a long way from the sort of car I usually liked to take racing, and my memory is that we had lots of problems and finally the gearbox broke. But according to the official records Jack and I finished fourth overall behind two Porsches and a Lotus, and won our class. So there you go.

↑ In March 1960 I was at Sebring to drive the Camoradi Birdcage Maserati in the 12 Hours, so when Donald Healey asked me to drive one of his Frogeye Sprites the day before in the four-hour supporting race for 1-litre cars, it sounded like fun. Being basically a production car, the Sprite had nothing like the pace of the 1-litre Abarths, but I led from the start and in the end I managed to finish second to the fastest of them.

📷 *Ozzie Lyons/www.petelyons.com*

➜ In 1961 Donald was determined to beat the Abarths, and laid on a four-car team with Bruce McLaren, Walt Hansgen, my sister Pat and me. We all had a great battle until clutch slip dropped me to fifth, but Walt won. In 1962 we were back for more, but this time Bruce and Walt had defected to Abarth.

The little Italian cars were a good 15mph quicker than the Sprites down the straight, but to my delight it rained before the race. In the conditions I was able to romp away, and at the end of lap 1 I led by 7 seconds. Then unfortunately the rain stopped, the circuit dried out, and coinciding with this my car developed fuel starvation and I had to pit for a top-up. So I finished third behind Bruce and Walt and ahead of two more Abarths. My team-mates Pedro Rodriguez and Innes Ireland – more Formula 1 drivers having fun in these little cars – were sixth and seventh.

📷 *Ozzie Lyons/www.petelyons.com*

9254 WD

← The Birdcage Maserati Tipo 60 was a fantastic car, and I simply loved it. My first race with it was a one-off for the works at Rouen in May 1959, when it was only a 2-litre. Maserati were almost bankrupt by then, but they still managed to produce this very clever machine, with its complex spaceframe of tiny tubes, very light and very rigid: it handled well and had excellent brakes. I had no problem leading from start to finish.

📷 *Klemantaski Collection*

⬇ By 1960 the Birdcage, now called the Tipo 61, was up to 2.8-litres, and it was a very competitive machine against the bigger Ferraris. Because of Maserati's financial troubles they couldn't afford to run a works team, but Lucky Casner's Camoradi outfit bought two cars and ran them in the white and blue US colours. Camoradi were a disorganised bunch, and in the Sebring 12 Hours, when I came in after my first stint to hand over to Dan Gurney, they had forgotten to tell him to get ready. That lost us some time, but he soon restored our lead and we were looking very comfortable when, with eight of the 12 hours gone, the transmission failed.

📷 *Stirling Moss collection*

⬆ I was back with Gurney in the Camoradi Birdcage for the 1960 Nürburgring 1000Kms. This was always one of my favourites – long race, long and demanding track, and very satisfying if you could do well. Having won it three times, I really wanted to get a fourth one.

After my complaints about Camoradi's organisation they got the veteran Italian Grand Prix driver Piero Taruffi to run our pit, which was a great improvement. But we had lots of problems in practice, so I was delighted to find when race day dawned that it was raining heavily, with thick fog.

It was like that the whole race, which helped me from the start to build up a big lead over the Ferraris and the very quick Bonnier/Gendebien Porsche. When I handed over to Dan he carried on the good work, until he came in with a ferocious oil leak around half-distance. An oil pipe had split, and it took an age to replace. Part of the problem was that it was so cold the oil pressure was higher than normal, which had burst the pipe, so while the pipe was replaced we taped over part of the oil cooler to raise the temperature.

📷 *Klemantaski Collection*

↓ Dan rejoined after a long delay and drove brilliantly to make up the deficit, working through the Ferraris and the Porsches and, after more than an hour's dedicated work, retaking the lead. This is Dan handing back to me for my last stint, and this stop dropped us back to third place again. But the Birdcage was going perfectly now, and its handling around the Nürburgring in the slippery conditions was all I could wish for. It took me five hard Nürburgring laps to get in front again, and in the end we won by nearly three minutes.

📷 *LAT*

← So I got my fourth Nürburgring 1000Kms win, and Dan's speed and consistency played a very big part. In my mind he is up there with Fangio and Tony Brooks as one of the three best co-drivers I ever worked with. 📷 *LAT*

⬇ Working on a shoestring, Maserati then developed a mid-engined version of the Birdcage, the Tipo 63. In theory, building on the success of the Tipo 61, it should have been a very effective weapon. This is the first prototype, which I tested at Modena early in 1961 in unfinished form, even before the Perspex screen had been made. It was finished, sort of, in time for Sebring in March, but when I tried it in practice it was far from race-ready: the handling was dreadful, and the rear suspension started to break up on the bumpy circuit. So for the race my co-driver that weekend, Graham Hill, and I opted for one of Camoradi's front-engined Tipo 61s. At the start the battery was flat, then the exhaust fell off. I took over the team's other car and the rear suspension collapsed. That was the sad end of my long and very enjoyable seven-year association with Maserati.

Getty Images

← A superb shot from the 1961 Targa Florio, clearly showing the character of the narrow 45-mile circuit of country roads around Sicily. Note the interesting gap in the wall and barrier on the left that is meant to protect cars from the sheer drop beyond – and the two policemen standing in the gap as I pass in my Porsche RS60 Spyder. Despite its lack of horsepower, it was an ideal car for the Targa's twists and bumps. Porsche had won the race in 1959 and '60, and I was hoping to make it three in a row for them.

I was paired with Graham Hill, and we had a torquier version of the flat-four engine in 2-litre spec rather than the normal 1700cc. For the 10-lap race we decided that I would do the first four laps and the last four, with Graham doing the two in the middle. We had the race in the bag, leading the von Trips/Phil Hill Ferrari by over a minute when, with 445 miles done and five to go to the finish, the differential failed.

📷 *LAT*

⬇ The Porsche Spyder was a wonderful giant-killer, and I was delighted to be asked by the factory to drive one in the Nürburgring 1000Kms, one of my favourite races, in 1961. This time we had the later model, the RS61, which normally ran in the 1600cc class, but to get it into the 2-litre class the engine had been stretched fractionally to 1630cc.

As usual I was hoping for bad 'Ring weather to be able to deal with the bigger cars, but to start with it was dry, although freezing cold. This shows me getting away first in the Le Mans start, from Phil Hill's Ferrari, Dan Gurney's Porsche and the Masten Gregory/Lucky Casner Camoradi Birdcage. I held the lead for a bit but I couldn't stay with the Ferraris. Then it did rain, and the rain quickly turned to snow, which helped me to get back up to second place, and soon I was closing on Phil. He later crashed, so this could have been another 'Ring win for me, but my engine blew up out in the country.

I got back to the pits on foot, and took over the Herbert Linge/Sepp Greger Porsche 356 Carrera. I caught Peter Lumsden's Lotus Elite to take the 2-litre sports car class lead, but he either didn't see me or didn't want to let me past, and I had to spin into the bank to avoid him. I carried on with the Carrera a bit dented, got past him, and won the class, finishing eighth overall. So the day wasn't completely wasted.

📷 *Stirling Moss collection*

← It was Cooper who first had the idea of widening one of their single-seater chassis, fitting it with an all-enveloping body, and racing it as a sports car. They called it the Cooper Monaco, and I bought one myself in 1959 and did three events in it before selling it on. Two of these were in Scandinavia, and the picture shows the Kannonloppet races at Karlskoga, which I won. It handled just like the Formula 1 car, except that in a straight line at high speeds it started to feel a little vague. We knew so little about aerodynamics then, and, with hindsight, I'm sure some sort of small spoiler at the front would have sorted that.

📷 *Stirling Moss collection*

← As had happened before, what Cooper did, Lotus copied and improved. Colin Chapman's answer to the Cooper Monaco was informally dubbed the Monte Carlo, although its official type was Lotus 19. Fitted with the full 2½-litre Climax engine, it was a brilliantly effective device. The first one made was taken over by British Racing Partnership – which about now, with sponsorship from United Dominions Trust, became the UDT-Laystall Racing Team – and was painted in the usual BRP pale green. The team then added two more, and I raced one whenever I could fit it into my calendar.

My first race in the Lotus 19 was also my first race after the Spa crash, at Karlskoga in Sweden. It had a Le Mans start, which was quite a test for my legs, which were both broken seven weeks earlier. After a brief battle with Jo Bonnier's Maserati I won, and decided I liked this car a lot.

I scored seven wins during 1960/61 with the UDT Lotus 19s, and in mid 1961, on a spare weekend between the Belgian and French Grands Prix, I hopped over to Canada for the Players 200 at Mosport. It was run in two heats, and I won both. Here I am on the grid before the start of the first heat.

📷 *Stirling Moss collection*

↑ I did several races in North America with the Lotus 19, and at the very nice Laguna Seca circuit in northern California I won their Pacific Grand Prix event two years running. They always gave me a friendly welcome there: one year somebody persuaded me to enhance my appearance with a Groucho Marx nose and glasses, and many thought it was quite an improvement.

📷 *Stirling Moss collection*

↑ At the 1961 Nassau races I drove a wire-wheeled customer Lotus 19 for the American Rosebud Racing Team, but I dropped out when a rear upright broke. Behind me is Jim Hall in the first front-engined Chaparral, built by Troutman & Barnes.

📷 *Stirling Moss collection*

↗ The first time I ever raced a Ferrari was in 1957 in the Nassau Trophy. I was meant to be driving a factory Aston DBR2, but it was loaned to Ruth Levy for the Ladies' race and she rolled it into a ball. I leave you to imagine what John Wyer said about that.

So the portly American enthusiast Temple Buell rented a Ferrari for me. It was a two-year-old single-cam 3½-litre V12 290S, tastefully turned out in purple and white, and it belonged to a Dutchman who rejoiced in the appropriate name, for a Ferrari owner, of Jan de Vroom. Initially I said I couldn't drive it because it had a centre throttle, but Mr de Vroom very decently had it converted overnight, all of which presumably went on Buell's hire car bill.

Compared to the Aston the brakes were feeble and the steering was heavy, and Jan was a different shape to me so I couldn't get comfortable. But at least the gearbox was better than the Aston's (which wasn't difficult). Despite the holiday atmosphere that always prevailed at Nassau, this was quite a serious 250-mile event, run at an average speed of over 101mph. I had a big battle with Masten Gregory in Buell's 450S Maserati until his transmission failed, and then with Carroll Shelby in John Edgar's 450S, before running out the winner from Carroll and Phil Hill's Ferrari 335S.

📷 *Stirling Moss collection*

→ I was a Ferrari man again in the 1962 Daytona Continental, a three-hour race that would eventually develop into the Daytona 24 Hours. I had already agreed with Enzo that I would be racing a Rob Walker blue Ferrari in Grands Prix that season, and there was also talk of a sports racer in UDT pale green, so my GT drive at Daytona was part of the developing Ferrari relationship. This was a NART-entered 250GT with very elegant Pininfarina bodywork, and it was a very nice motor car. Not only did I win the GT category by three laps, but I also finished fourth overall behind the likes of Dan Gurney's Lotus 19, Phil Hill's Ferrari 206S and Jim Hall's Chaparral. Running on both the Daytona banking and on the infield circuit was reminiscent of, but different from, Monza. This shot is taken on the infield, with Buck Fulp's NART Ferrari following.

📷 *Getty Images*

➜ At the Daytona Continental and feeling part of the Ferrari family already, I chat to Phil Hill as I sit nonchalantly on the front wing of his 206S. On the left is Olivier Gendebien, who, like me, was racing a 250GT.

📷 *Getty Images*

⬇ My last-ever endurance sports car race was the 1962 Sebring 12 Hours, and Innes Ireland and I were in a NART-entered Ferrari TR61 – actually the car that had won Le Mans the year before. By half-distance we were leading by two laps, and Innes and I felt sure that the race would be ours. But unfortunately NART's sheer incompetence cost us victory. They had eight cars in the race, their pit was a shambles, nobody had even looked at the race rules, and nobody was keeping a proper lap chart. In the chaos our Testa Rossa was refuelled too early, and to our disgust we were disqualified.

📷 *Ozzie Lyons/www.petelyons.com*

→ Archie Scott Brown used to get astonishing lap times out of the light and sweet-handling Lister-Jaguars. Two months after his tragic death at Spa in May 1958 Brian Lister asked me to handle his car, wearing the famous Cambridge registration MVE 303, in the British Grand Prix support race. I liked it very much, and had a start-to-finish win. My pole position time was 1m 44s, which would have put me on the fifth row of the grid for the Grand Prix that afternoon.

📷 *Ferret Fotographics*

⬇ Although I used to race the big Mk VII saloons in the early 1950s when I was a Jaguar works driver, I rather missed out on the growth of touring car racing, but I had a one-off drive in Tommy Sopwith's Equipe Endeavour 3.8 Mk 2 at the 1960 May Silverstone. The Mk 2 was very quick for a four-door saloon, but a lot more nervous on the limit than the lumbering, friendly old Mk VII had been. I managed to get pole ahead of Roy Salvadori in the white John Coombs 3.8, but he made the better start. I got past him at Stowe on lap 2, but on lap 9 I was baulked momentarily on the Hangar Straight by a backmarker and he went ahead. It was a great battle, and Roy won it fair and square.

📷 *Stirling Moss collection*

← In 1956 the six-cylinder Austin-Healey 100-Six replaced the old 100-4, and Donald Healey built up a special long-nosed version for record attempts on the Bonneville Salt Flats, reaching 152mph. He then brought the car to Nassau that December, and I practised it on the Oakes Field airfield circuit, but I didn't race it.

📷 *Stirling Moss collection*

← This curious little machine is a Micromill, which was raced on French indoor dirt tracks. One evening in 1959 the promoters organised a celebrity event in Paris and asked several Formula 1 drivers to join in. It was just a bit of fun. There were three heats and a final: I won two heats and then in the third my back axle broke. In the final I had a battle with Harry Schell until he hit the straw bales and I turned over. I ran across to another car, rejoined in that, and finished second. After all that they decided I was first overall, but I have no idea why.

📷 *Stirling Moss collection*

➜ If I had been born 40 years later, I suppose I would have been learning on karts rather than learning on horses. Mike Keele, an old friend who had an engineering business in Tring, produced the Keelekart, and here I am about to try one out in Nassau.

At that time the most basic karts had no gearbox or clutch, with one or two engines (100cc Class 1 or 200cc Class 2) driving the back wheels directly by chain. The more sophisticated 200cc Class 4 karts boasted a clutch and a motorcycle gearbox, like this Villiers-powered machine. Its substantial construction and hefty steering wheel show that it dates back to the early days of karts: before long they were much smaller, lighter and neater. There's no doubt that karting has played its part in teaching succeeding generations a lot about wheel-to-wheel racing.

📷 *Getty Images*

➜ This has to be one of the more unusual single-seaters that I tried. I never raced it: indeed it never raced. It is CERV-1, standing for Chevrolet Engineering Research Vehicle 1. It was built by General Motors in 1959 under the direction of Zora Arkus-Duntov, who was responsible for the race development of the Corvette. It was supposed to have been built so that Chevrolet could test various components that might eventually find their way onto production cars, but I suspect it was more a show car than anything else. It had a small-block Chevy V8 in the back, and very nice styling and paintwork, but it was far too heavy for a racing car, and drove rather like a road car. But it was nice of the guys at GM to let me have a go.

📷 *Stirling Moss collection*

CHAPTER 12
HOW IT ALL CHANGED

Easter Monday, 23 April 1962: the day my professional racing career ended, and the day my life very nearly ended. The annoying thing is, I have no memory of any of it.

Every night before I went to sleep, year in year out, I would scribble a quick summary of what I'd been up to in a day-to-a-page diary. I still have all those diaries and, along with my memories of the time, they have been the basis that Simon and I have used to write this book. Sometimes the entries are brief; sometimes they are quite detailed, specifying lap times or gear ratio changes. Even the night of my 1960 Spa accident I managed to write: 'Shunt. Nose. Back. Legs. Bruises. Bugger!'

But my diary entries end abruptly on Sunday 22 April. I know I spent the night at The Fleece, which was the Chichester pub where I often stayed before a Goodwood meeting. Practice for the Bank Holiday Monday Goodwood meetings was always on the Saturday, and it was raining hard when we set our grid times for Monday's Formula 1 race, the 100-mile Glover Trophy, which I had won twice before. I took pole in the Lotus 18/21, now run by BRP in their pale green UDT colours because Rob Walker's workshop had been cleared to await the arrival of the Ferrari. Graham Hill's new stack-pipe BRM V8 and Bruce McLaren's Cooper were next up.

My road car at the time was a Lotus Elite, and my only memory of Monday is that, as I left The Fleece car park, I damaged the exhaust on a wooden block that the gates closed onto, and that annoyed me. The rest of the day is a complete blank, and I don't really have any memories until six weeks later. Reading the contemporary reports of the Glover Trophy, I see that I was having problems from the start, and after nine laps I came in to have the gear linkage adjusted. I rejoined a long way down.

Hill was leading comfortably from McLaren, and in that comparatively short race I had no hope of making up the two laps I had lost. But it was always my philosophy to keep racing as long as I had a car under me: I believed I had that duty to the spectators, who had paid to see us in action, and maybe I could end the day with a new lap record. Sure enough, I did set a new outright lap record (also equalled by John Surtees' Lola), and by lap 30 of the 42 I was back up to seventh place. On lap 35 I came up behind Graham's BRM, ready to unlap myself. As we approached the right-hand section of St Mary's I was on the left of the road, almost alongside Graham – and I shot across the grass and hit the bank head-on.

I, and many others, have speculated endlessly about why I did that. Maybe I thought Graham was letting me through, and then I realised he was going to move across me to take his line. Maybe Graham acknowledged the blue flag he was being given with a hand signal to the marshal, and I thought he was waving me through. Maybe there was some sort of mechanical failure – I had suffered a sticking throttle in a race the week before at Snetterton – but such examination as was possible of the wreckage does not point to this.

The photographs that were taken after the accident, with me trapped in the car, look rather lurid, but in fact I find myself able to look at them quite dispassionately. After all, I knew nothing about it. I was trapped in the car for about 45 minutes, I gather, because the chassis had completely folded up over me. Fortunately there was no fire. With huge pipe-cutters they cut the chassis tubes and got me out, and I was taken to Chichester Hospital and then on to the Atkinson Morley in Wimbledon. I didn't begin to regain consciousness for 38 days.

I was almost alongside him – and I shot across the grass and hit the bank. I, and many others, have speculated endlessly about why I did that.

I had pretty serious brain injuries, and my face was badly crushed, particularly the left eye socket and cheekbone. My left arm and leg were broken, the leg in two places. I was paralysed down one side for a while, and when I started to wake up I didn't know how to speak. There were various other bits and pieces to be dealt with. Fortunately – this was the first thing I asked the doctors when I was awake enough to think about it – my old man was all right.

As I started to recover, all my motivation, of course, was to try to get everything healed up as fast as possible. The surgeons, doctors and staff at the Atkinson Morley were just wonderful, and as well as everything else they had to put up with journalists and photographers camped outside, trying to get in. I left hospital, on crutches, on 22 June, which was nearly nine weeks after the accident. Having taken out for the evening all the nurses who had looked after me so well, I flew to Nassau to recuperate in my house there. Several months later I flew back to have my eye socket rebuilt, which was done with bone taken from my hip, and there were follow-up procedures too.

Of course what everybody – journalists, media, friends – wanted to know, as did I more than anyone else, was this: would I race again? There was a lot of pressure on me to make a decision. So on 1 May 1963, a Wednesday, I drove myself down to Goodwood and got into the BRP Lotus 19. It had been raining and the track was quite wet. I had a faint hope, as I went through the right-hand sweep into St Mary's, that I might remember something, but there was nothing. It was just a corner. My lap times were perfectly good in the conditions, and I certainly wasn't off the pace.

But it was all different. I had always driven a racing car almost instinctively: the car was an extension of myself, and I went through all the motions without deliberate thought – positioning the car exactly where I wanted to be on the track, correcting a slide, changing gear at precisely the right revs, hitting each braking point. I just did it, in a sort of joyous flow. Now I had to think what I was doing.

As I lapped the circuit my brain was consciously having to pick up messages from the car and send them to my hands and feet. I had to tell myself what to do. Before, I knew where the rev-counter needle was pointing without taking my eyes off the track: I could just assimilate that information, as well as information from my mirrors or from the weather conditions in the sky, without looking at them. I could even take note of a friendly photographer at the apex of a corner and give him a wave, all while setting a pole-position time. But now all that had gone. I brought the car into the pits, got out, and said: 'I have retired.'

Now, looking back, I realise that I did that trial run much too soon. Although my bones had healed, my brain had not properly recovered from its injuries. Had I set up that test two years after the accident, or even longer, the story might have been different. When I had my accident I was 32 years old, and I had been racing for 14 years. I was driving as well as I had ever done, maybe better. Had the accident not happened I firmly believe I would have continued for at least another 14 years, and probably much more.

Instead, having lived a rarefied existence since my late teens, I would have to join the real world. It had been an enormous privilege to race the best cars, for the best teams, against the best drivers in the world. Now it was time to earn my living, like anybody else.

← Easter Monday, 1962: in the paddock during the morning, somebody photographed me checking the oil on my Lotus Elite road car. The nose of the Lotus 18/21 is in the background.

📷 *sutton-images.com*

→ On the grid, in pole position for the last race of my professional career. Everything totally normal: Herbert Johnson helmet, clean blue Dunlop overalls with sewn-on BRDC badge, string-back leather gloves, goggles with black tape across the top to cut down glare, spare goggles slung around my neck.

📷 *sutton-images.com*

→ Coming through the Goodwood chicane and going well after my pitstop, I have just unlapped my UDT-Laystall team-mate Innes Ireland in the four-cylinder Lotus-Climax 21. He finished third.

📷 *Getty Images*

↑ The accident has just happened, and marshals and a St John Ambulance man have rushed to my aid. Hurrying up on the left is a young St John Ambulance nurse.

📷 *Getty Images*

→ They have got my crash helmet off and the St John Ambulance nurse is holding my hand while the others try to work out how they can get me out. I am totally unconscious, of course. The nurse's name, I discovered later, was Annie Strudwick, and she was 19 years old. I was able to write and thank her, and almost half a century later she was my guest at the Goodwood Revival.

📷 *Getty Images*

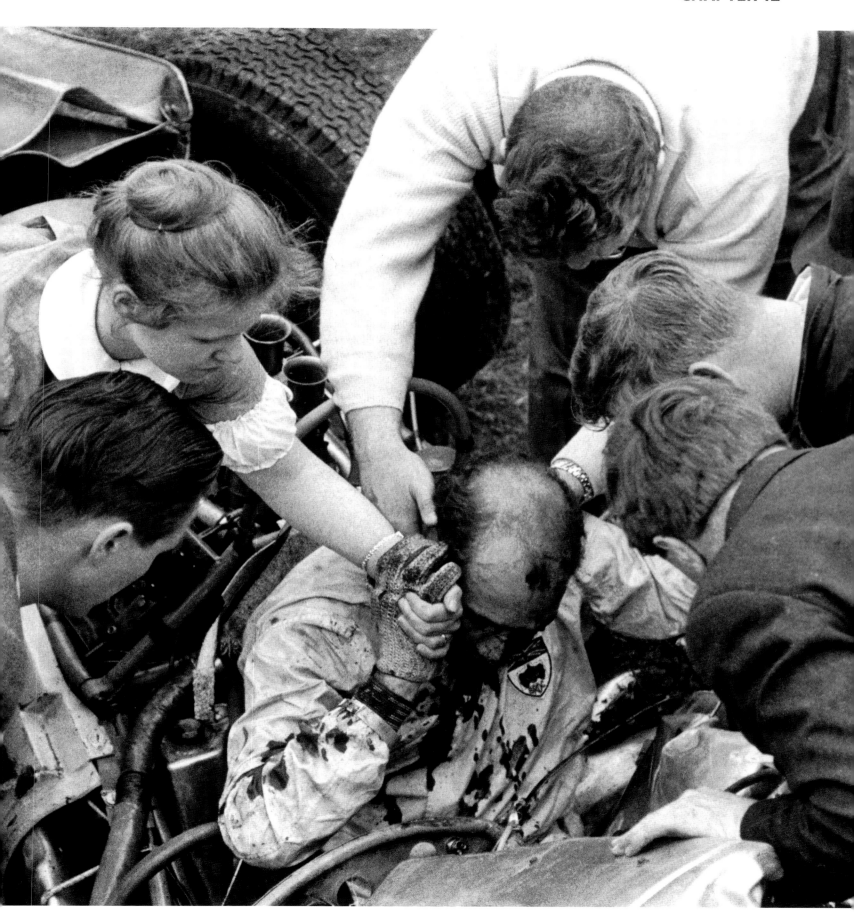

← My poor old Lotus 18/21 was pretty comprehensively shortened in the accident, and looking at this shot I can understand why it took them 45 minutes to get me out. I'm very glad it didn't catch fire.

📷 *Getty Images*

← It was a long time before I was able to sit up in a chair, and even then I still wasn't really functioning properly. Here my long-suffering Mum is serving me breakfast. While I was still unconscious she sat by my bed for hours, reading some of the pile of get-well letters out loud in case I could hear them.

📷 *Stirling Moss collection*

→ When I had made enough progress to be wheeled around the hospital grounds, I was already working my hands and arms, trying to get my co-ordination back.

📷 *TopFoto*

← On 22 June 1962, eight weeks and five days after the accident, with the help of crutches I'm able to walk out of the Atkinson Morley Hospital. Mum is on the left of the picture, and over my right shoulder, looking cheerful because of my progress, is my good friend David Haynes.
📷 *Getty Images*

→ During the long weeks in the Atkinson Morley the nurses who looked after me were friendly, patient and very good at their job. I said 'thank you' to them by taking them out to dinner, and then on to the Criterion Theatre to see a show. This was taken in the Criterion bar.
📷 *Getty Images*

→ On a wet day at Goodwood in May 1963, I bring the Lotus 19 back into the paddock having reeled off a good quantity of laps and made my tough but inevitable decision: retirement. But if I had resisted the pressure of everyone who was clamouring for me to make up my mind, and maybe given my brain another year to heal, that decision might have been different.
📷 *Rex Features*

CHAPTER 13
BACK TO WORK

Following my accident and during my long period of recuperation, everybody was very kind. I had shoals of letters, from people I knew and people I didn't, wishing me well. I even got a letter from Frank Sinatra. There was much more media attention than I'd bargained for, and some of it applied the pressure that persuaded me, as recounted in the last chapter, to have that Goodwood try-out too early.

But at least it meant that, despite not being a racing driver any more, the world hadn't completely forgotten about me yet. That helped me to start earning a living – and, I'm happy to say, it still does. A lot of my energies were devoted to building up a London property portfolio, but I was able to continue working around motor racing, doing presentational work, PR, and some TV commentary.

All this began even before I'd announced my retirement. In February 1963 I flew to Sydney to attend the Australian Grand Prix at Warwick Farm. Meanwhile BP, who had backed me throughout my racing career, were reorganising their retail network, and I found myself opening garages up and down the country. Later I was crossing the Atlantic a lot, because Johnson Wax were sponsoring the new Canadian-American Challenge Series, the CanAm, and hired me to help promote it. It provided great racing with those big V8 Group 7 cars, and because it had a very good purse quite a few of the top Formula 1 racers – Bruce, Denny, John Surtees, later Jackie Stewart – took part. I was also team manager for the *Sunday Times*-sponsored AC Cobra that finished seventh at Le Mans in 1963.

That year I founded SMART, the Stirling Moss Automobile Racing Team, and through the '60s we fielded lots of machinery in the team's pale green colours. First came a Lotus Elan 26R with aerodynamic tweaks by Frank Costin

that was successfully raced by John Whitmore. I also helped Hugh Dibley with his Brabham BT8, and Charlie Crichton-Stuart with his F3 Brabham. There was a Triumph Spitfire that was rallied by my PA Val Pirie, and then I bought a Porsche 904 that was raced by Whitmore, Innes Ireland, Trevor Taylor, David Hobbs and others. In the 1970s visiting Brazilian Formula Ford racers Luiz Bueno and Ricardo Achcar raced under the SMART banner, and Luiz later went very well in his homeland, winning the Brazilian championship in a Porsche 908 and even doing a couple of F1 races.

I got involved in various businesses. An interesting one was the Stirling Moss Paint-a-Car System, which was an idea a Canadian chap came up with. It was a way of getting your car resprayed quickly and cheaply using a quick-drying acrylic paint, and we franchised a string of centres in the UK and a couple in Paris and Belgium.

As soon as I got back to normal health, and shaved off the beard that was hiding the scars until they healed, I started to get offers and opportunities to get behind the wheel again. But I resisted them. I suppose the first time I relented was in 1968, when I was asked to take part in the Marathon de la Route, 84 hours of racing around the full Nürburgring. It was wonderful to reacquaint myself with one of my all-time favourite circuits, and it felt as though I had never been away. With my co-drivers Innes Ireland and Umberto Maglioli we got past all the Porsches and into the lead, before the gearbox broke – that was just like old times, too.

In 1974 I did the World Cup Rally, a mad event that went across the Sahara Desert to Nigeria and back. We were in a factory-prepared Mercedes 280E saloon, and we ended up deep in the desert with a broken gearbox and not much water, so that was a bit of a drama – although the London

1963 ONWARDS
As soon as I got back to normal health I started to get offers and opportunities to get back behind the wheel again.

papers blew it up into much more than it was. In 1976 I did the Bathurst 1000, Australia's most famous touring car race, with Jack Brabham in a Holden Torana. That one started badly when Jack got shunted on the starting grid, and it didn't get much better, but after a long rebuild in the pits we got back in the race, and Jack and I had a good go.

On the personal front I married again, an American girl called Elaine Barbarino, but the only really good thing to come out of that was my daughter, Allison. She's a great girl, happily married to a very decent chap, and has produced my three grandchildren.

After Elaine and I divorced I became a bachelor again for some 10 years, with all the advantages and a few of the disadvantages that entails. Then I met Susie – or actually re-met her, because I had known her all her life. When she was growing up in Hong Kong her father was a good friend, and I used to stay with him when I was travelling through. Soon Susie and I started seeing more of each other. In 1980 we were married, and soon after our son Elliot was born.

In 1980 I signed with Audi to do a couple of seasons in the British Touring Car Championship. I didn't enjoy it much: touring car racing, on slicks, had become something of a contact sport by then. Much more my cup of tea was historic racing, which started to gather momentum in the late 1970s.

My first foray was in one of the supporting events at the 1977 British Grand Prix. I drove a Maserati 250F, just like the cars I had been racing in the World Championship two decades before, and it was a wonderful experience. That led me into all sorts of cars that I had raced, or raced against, in period: a Birdcage Maserati at Laguna Seca, an Aston DBR1 at Goodwood, Irvine Laidlaw's glorious Ferrari GTO, at the Monaco Historics a C-type Jaguar and a Frazer-Nash Le Mans

Replica like the ones I raced there in 1952. All that was hugely enjoyable for me.

I also drove lots of historic racers that post-dated my retirement: like a GT40 at Watkins Glen, and the Shelby Mustang with which I won my class down-under in the Targa Tasmania. I did the Playboy Series in America in the 1980s in a Brumos Porsche, sharing with Innes, and I enjoyed myself in an Alfa TZ. Then there was an Elva-BMW Mk 7, which I had sprayed in Rob Walker blue, plus a Lotus 23B and Chevrons B8, B16 and B19. There were too many to list them all, but I have to mention the Mille Miglia: no longer the real race, of course, but a very enjoyable three-day rally. I have done it many times in my original Mercedes, loaned by the factory museum and still wearing its number 722. On the 40th anniversary of my victory I took my friend Simon Taylor: I have to say his navigation wasn't in the Jenks class, but I think he enjoyed his time in the SLR's passenger seat.

Several of these cars I bought myself, like my Lola Mk 1, my Osca, and a Porsche Spyder similar to the car that nearly won me the 1961 Targa Florio. It was in the Porsche that I made a momentous decision – momentous for me, anyway.

I'd entered it for the historic race preceding the 2011 Le Mans 24 Hours, a race I'd done and enjoyed several times in the past. But during practice it suddenly hit me that I wasn't enjoying it any more. I only ever wanted to drive at a speed that would be competitive with everybody else, and give me a chance of doing really well. But now I realised that if I drove fast enough to beat people I thought I ought to beat, I would scare myself. All through my career, I'd never been scared racing a car. But you have to be honest about these things. So I came into the pits, and I said, 'That's it'. At 81 years and 9 months, I had retired – again.

➔ Having become an ordinary working man, I had to spend much more time at my desk than I'd been used to. But I never had any difficulty finding myself extremely busy: my property activities, various business ideas, PR work, public speaking, appearances of one sort or another, a bit of racing driver management. I can truthfully say there hasn't been a dull moment in the past 50-plus years.

📷 *LAT*

← I have never liked big vehicles in London, and object to paying parking fees. My scooter was my transport of choice, and it was ideal for travelling around my properties to collect rents or see to leaking taps. To my great relief, helmets were not legally required then. When they did become mandatory in 1973, I wore a white Herbert Johnson, of course.

📷 *Stirling Moss collection*

➔ SMART – the Stirling Moss Automobile Racing Team – was quite active in the 1960s. This is our Lotus Elan 26R with aerodynamic modifications by Frank Costin, including contoured screen and roof, and smaller air intake. During the 1963 season John Whitmore made it go very fast, when it held together.

📷 *LAT*

➜ Of course I kept up with everything that was happening with my old friends in the motor racing world. Here I am at Warwick Farm in February 1963 – actually three months before that Goodwood test that persuaded me to retire. Jack Brabham has just won the Australian Grand Prix in his Brabham, and I'm helping out with the presentations.

📷 *LAT*

↑ The Monaco Grand Prix has always attracted lots of celebrities. In 1966, when the race was won by Jackie Stewart's BRM, I bumped into Steve McQueen and we reminisced about racing Sprites at Sebring (see pages 262 and 264).

📷 *Getty Images*

↗ My long-time friend, roguish Shepherds Bush car dealer Cliff Davis, was keen to promote midget racing on stadium ovals in the UK, and he let me have a go. The adhesion was minimal even at low speeds, so you could have a lot of fun going sideways.

📷 *Paul Skilleter*

→ Get a few old racing drivers together and you can't stop them trying to beat each other, even if the vehicles are dodgem cars at Battersea Fun Fair. On the left, 1967 World Champion Denny Hulme; on the right, 1964 World Champion John Surtees; in the middle yours truly, with HJ helmet of course.

📷 *Getty Images*

← In 1968 I had my first taste of competing on a circuit for more than six years, and on one my favourite circuits at that. The Marathon de la Route, once a famous long-distance rally that ran from Liège to Sofia and back, had now become an 84-hour blind around the Nürburgring, and for this event I fixed up a drive in a works Lancia Fulvia with two good old boys of my generation, Innes Ireland and Umberto Maglioli. The race used not only the familiar 14.2-mile Nordschleife but also the Sudschleife loop as well, making 17½ miles in all, and started at 1am on the Wednesday, running without stopping until 1pm on Saturday. There were lots of serious Porsche 911s entered, but when I had my first stint at 7pm on Wednesday I found it just felt natural to slip into a rhythm, and soon I was lapping quicker than all the Porsches. By Thursday morning we were leading, even though in the middle of the night Innes only just missed a deer that came bounding out of the forest. Then, while Umberto was at the wheel, the gearbox seized. But while it lasted it had been great fun.

📷 *Stirling Moss collection*

← The Marathon organisers laid on Fangio, who happened to be in Europe at the time, to flag us away at 1am. Of all the friendships that I made in my 14 years of full-time racing, the most special was with him, my team leader and mentor at Mercedes in 1955, and the man I always respected more than any other in motor racing. When he greeted me the years rolled away.

📷 *Getty Images*

⬆ In the days when the British Grand Prix was held on a Saturday, there used to be a cricket match on the Sunday, and in 1968 it was held on the Mersham, Kent, pitch between Lord Brabourne's XI and a motley gathering of at least 15 racing drivers who made up Les Leston's XI. Some of them were new to cricket: Pedro Rodriguez seemed pretty bemused by it all, and Jochen Rindt's method of bowling had more to do with rocket-launchers than with The Oval.

The fact that the umpires were racing people – Colin Chapman, Mike Parkes and Peter Proctor – should have given our side an advantage, but there were some proper cricketers on the other side, and they trounced us. They had HRH Prince Charles on their side, and he was pretty useful, despatching both Piers Courage and our captain Denny Hulme. But Bruce McLaren managed a brilliant catch that sent the heir to the throne back to the pavilion.

This team photograph shows that Formula 1 drivers knew how to relax in those days. Standing, from left, are Les Leston, Richard Attwood, Piers Courage, Jochen Rindt, Graham Hill, Pedro Rodriguez, Denny Hulme, Rob Widdows, Peter Procter and Peter Jopp. Kneeling, from left, are Innes Ireland, Bruce McLaren, Chris Amon, me and Colin Chapman. I can't see the current F1 grid finding time to play a jokey cricket match together…

📷 *LAT*

← The 1976 Formula 1 season, and the tense battle for the title between James Hunt and Niki Lauda, had us all going, but James and Niki were friendly and good-humoured about it all the way. The long hair identifies Jackie Stewart, with his back to the camera.
📷 *LAT*

← This is Elliot Moss at his christening, with his proud parents. When he was born I got a congratulatory telegram from Enzo Ferrari that said: 'Happy birthday young Stirling, future champion of the world.' Later, when we were passing near Maranello, we went to see Enzo, and he offered to hold Elliot while we took a picture of young Moss in his arms – so that in years to come he can show that he once met Signor Ferrari. Enzo was a tough, ruthless old man, but underneath all that I think somewhere there was a soft heart.

Elliot is now 34, happily married to Helen, and a professional-standard chef, having worked under Michel Roux Jr at Le Gavroche. He now runs my property business.
📷 *Stirling Moss collection*

➜ In 1974 Mercedes-Benz supplied me with a factory-prepared 280E to do the World Cup Rally, a wild 11,000-mile event through 14 countries that started in London, went down through North Africa and across the Sahara Desert to Nigeria, then back up again to Germany. I took former Lotus racer Mike Taylor with me, and the picture shows us on a test run around the military proving ground at Bagshot. The event ended badly for us: somewhere in the Sahara, with damaged suspension and a leaking gearbox, we struggled to a French Foreign Legion fort, only to find it abandoned and deserted. The tabloid press trumpeted stories that said we were missing, presumed goodness knows what, and it's true that when somebody finally came to get us we only had half a day's water left. So we were quite relieved when they hove into view. No sat-nav in those days…

 *Ferret Fotographics*

➜ Jack Brabham asked me to share a Holden Torana with him in the 1976 Bathurst 1000, on the Mount Panorama circuit west of Sydney. I was looking forward to this 620-mile race because the circuit is hilly and very demanding, but on the grid Jack found his gearbox jammed, couldn't get a gear, and was rammed hard from behind by a Triumph Dolomite. It took the Holden crew 71 laps to rebuild the back end, but we thought we should still put on a show so we rejoined the race. But the only diff they'd been able to find for the rebuild made the car ferociously under-geared, so inevitably after another 37 laps it dropped a valve.

Stirling Moss collection

➜ In 1980 I signed a two-year deal with Audi to race in the British Touring Car Championship. I wasn't at all suited to this type of racing. Slick tyres seemed to reward fistful driving rather than fingertip driving – more for people who had taken their early lessons behind the wheel of a kart rather than holding the reins of a horse. Also, I wasn't used to motor racing being a contact sport. In my day there were no seat belts or roll cages. If you drove into somebody else and caused an accident you could very seriously injure either the other guy, or yourself. But in 1980s touring cars, clouting the other chap was part of normal racing. The only time I really enjoyed it was when it rained, because on a wet track treaded tyres replaced the slicks, and sensitive car control got better results.

BRDC Archive

⬆ In 1983 I told Bernie Ecclestone, who then owned and ran the Brabham Grand Prix team, that I would be interested to know what 800 turbocharged horsepower felt like. He responded by laying on a test session on the Brands Hatch short circuit in a BT52-BMW, like the one Nelson Piquet was using to win that year's World Championship. When I turned up with my Dunlop overalls and my Herbert Johnson the Brabham boys were a bit taken aback, but I told them that was how I'd always dressed to drive a racing car and I wasn't about to change now.

When I had wriggled down into the cockpit I was quite comfortable, and until you really tried to approach the limit the car was quite easy to drive with the huge grip from those big slicks. But the power was simply unbelievable. When the turbo came in at around 8000rpm it made the whole car feel like it was going into orbit. I was enjoying myself so much that I stayed out a long time, and after 40 laps I spun at what we used to call Kidney Bend. But I carried on, and in all I did 60 laps, getting down to a best of 46.6s. They told me Nigel Mansell had done a test there a few weeks before and done a 41.1s, so I reckoned that 5.5 seconds off the pace wasn't too bad in a completely strange type of car against somebody who drove one all the time. Thank you, Bernie.

📷 *LAT*

→ This event was the 75th anniversary of the founding of the Boy Scout movement, now called the Scout Association. I don't remember what the criteria for inclusion in this photo were, but making the salute are Derek Nimmo, Frankie Howerd, David Bellamy, me and Frank Bough. I don't think any of us could have lit a fire by rubbing two sticks together.

Getty Images

→ Wide wheels and slicks, seat belts and rollover bars weren't really what I wanted to play with, but when historic racing started to gather momentum I knew it would suit me much better. I think my first historic race was at Silverstone in the race supporting the 1977 British Grand Prix. I drove Neil Corner's later-type Maserati 250F, like the one I'd used to win the Italian Grand Prix 21 years earlier. At this stage I wasn't allowed to wear my old Herbert Johnson helmet, but in the end the FIA President, Max Mosley, gave special dispensation for me to race in my HJ hat, my blue Dunlop overalls, and without seat belts. After all, the only head that was going to get hurt was my own.

BRDC Archive

← This was a British Grand Prix support race too, at Brands Hatch in 1980. The car is Anthony Bamford's flawless recreation of a 1960 Ferrari Dino 246, just like Phil's and Taffy's and Ritchie's.
🅾 *LAT*

↓ At the 2008 Goodwood Revival it was great to remind myself what it was like racing a big old Jaguar Mk VII like the ones I drove at Silverstone in the early 1950s. Hustling through the chicane, it was just as I remembered: it handled really rather well.
🅾 *LAT*

→ I always loved small 1950s sports-racing cars, and after enjoying myself in historic racing in a Widi and a Lola Mk 1, I bought this beautiful little Osca FS372. I also persuaded Alfieri Maserati to sell me the only desmodromic head in existence for its 1500 twin-cam engine. Here I am taking the flag at the 2010 Goodwood Revival.
📷 *LAT*

⬇ Having fond memories of the Porsche Spyder RS60 with which I so nearly won the 1961 Targa Florio, I got hold of a similar car of my own. Here I am at the Goodwood Festival of Speed, and it's typical of the attention to detail by Lord March and his team that I'm number 136, just as I was in the '61 Targa.
📷 *LAT*

CHAPTER 14
IN CONCLUSION

Looking back over this book, I realise I have led a charmed life. I've been able to spend the first 30 years or so doing what I loved to do, and most of the time getting pretty well paid for it. For the next 50 I've had a hectic, busy time and a lot of fun, and I am still having that.

My philosophy all that time has been: Movement is Tranquillity. I don't know where I first read that; maybe I made it up myself. But it describes very well my approach to each day. I don't feel tranquil unless I am rushing about. I have never been any good at doing nothing. Even when I was a child I couldn't sit still: I wanted to find something or somebody to compete with. I have always wanted to find ways to cram more into each day, and now that I'm 85 it's no different. Motor racing is all about extracting the maximum out of each second, each fraction of a second. You do all you can to reduce how long you spend doing anything: if you reduce your lap time from 1min 24.38sec to 1min 24.13sec, you have extracted another quarter of a second in which to live your life.

If you've read thus far, you will have realised that things were very different then from how they are today. We raced on real roads, with trees, buildings, walls, hills and steep drops. We didn't have artificial tracks laid out with run-off areas and barriers, and we didn't have seat belts or roll-over bars. It was much more dangerous then, of course, and I lost far too many good friends. But it was the danger itself, as well as the demanding nature of the tracks, that distinguished the men who were racers from the men who were just drivers. I raced cars because it was a challenge, and in the challenge, like it or not, was the danger.

Today's F1 drivers aren't mates with each other. They are too much tucked up in their motorhomes, they're too much controlled by their managers, they can't misbehave because the sponsors wouldn't like it. You can't imagine a bunch of them meeting up for dinner after qualifying. No cayenne pepper in anyone's pyjamas. When I was racing we really were friends. You've only got to look at some of the photos in this book to see that. I think what drew us together was the danger: the unspoken factor that we all understood, that death might be around the next corner.

Today's top drivers now earn incomprehensible sums of money – one or two of them half a million pounds a week. At the height of my career I felt I was well-paid, but no more than if I had been, say, a top barrister or an eminent surgeon. But I'm absolutely certain of one thing: for me, my era was the best era, and I am very glad I raced when I did.

At the end of the 1950s I bought the freehold of a bombsite in a small cul-de-sac in Mayfair, just off Park Lane, and while I was on a long flight to Australia – making use of the time, you see – I sketched out my ideal house. I have lived there for over 50 years now, and as well as being my home it is my hub, my centre of operations. I have never wanted to live anywhere else, although I do have a holiday home in the USA. But the idea of living in Switzerland or Monaco or anywhere else to avoid paying tax is an anathema to me. I am British, and I am happy to pay my dues to help my country turn its wheels.

Road cars are no longer of interest to me, because in London parking is a nightmare. So I think small. I have an Aston Martin Cygnet – that's Susie's, really – and I have my Renault Twizy, plugged into the mains in the garage inside my house so it is always ready to go. It's 8½ feet long and 4 feet wide, no road tax, no congestion charge.

I love gadgets, and my house is full of them, for their ingenuity, and also – if they are any good – because they can save time. In the kitchen we can get fizzy water straight from one tap, and instant boiling water from another.

→ Susie and me enjoying a laugh at the Goodwood Revival. I can't imagine how I could cram in all the commitments I still have without her helping to make everything happen. We work together as a team, always.

📷 *Daimler Archive*

A gadget can go wrong, of course. I have a lift in my house, and one day in March 2010 I opened the doors and the lift wasn't there. I fell three floors down the lift shaft into the basement, shattered both my ankles and chipped three vertebrae. I was back to the old task of mending myself after injury, crutches and physio and all that, and when you're 80 it all takes a bit longer. But I was racing my Osca at the Goodwood Revival that September.

This is where I have to acknowledge that I simply could not operate without Susie. She looks after me, organises me, travels with me on all my working trips around the world, knows where I have to be at any time, and never loses her sense of humour, even if I lose mine. She makes sure that my life works. Susie and I have been together for 38 years and married for 35, and she has never stopped being the best thing that ever happened to me.

As I said: a charmed life.

INDEX